PAGANS
AND THE
LAW

Understand Your Rights

PAGANS
AND THE
LAW

Understand Your Rights

DANA D. EILERS

Attorney and Pagan Activist

New Page BOOKS

A DIVISION OF THE CAREER PRESS, INC.
FRANKLIN LAKES, NJ

PAGANS AND THE LAW
EDITED BY LAUREN MANOY
TYPESET BY STACEY A. FARKAS
Cover design by Cheryl Cohan Finbow
Printed in the U.S.A. by Book-mart Press

To order this title, please call toll-free 1-800-CAREER-1 (NJ and Canada: 201-848-0310) to order using VISA or MasterCard, or for further information on books from Career Press.

This book provides information about the law merely designed to help readers understand their own legal needs. But legal information is not the same as legal advice—the application of law to an individual's specific circumstances. Accordingly, the contents of this publication are intended as general legal information only and should not form the basis for legal advice of any kind. Professional legal advice should be sought and/or taken before any course of action is pursued.

The Career Press, Inc., 3 Tice Road, PO Box 687,
Franklin Lakes, NJ 07417
www.careerpress.com
www.newpagebooks.com

Library of Congress Cataloging-in-Publication Data
Eilers, Dana D.
    Pagans and the law : understand your rights / by Dana Eilers.
        p. cm.
    Includes bibliographical references and index.
    ISBN 1-56414-671-5 (pbk.)
        1. Neopagans—Legal status, laws, etc.—United States. I. Title.

KF4869.N45E38 2003
342.73'0852—dc21   2003048785

DEDICATION

This book is dedicated to my father, who always wondered what I did in my copious spare time.

ACKNOWLEDGMENTS

It seems that good friends of mine are always biting off things for me to chew on. When I came to Massachusetts in search of another life in the spring of 2000, I met with someone I had known from the Internet and from various Pagan e-mail lists. I drove from Cape Cod up to Salem and had lunch with Jerrie Hildebrand who asked me, "Dana, when are you going to write a book about Pagans and the law?"

I looked at her like she had a few wands loose.

I said, "Jerrie, who wants to read some dusty and boring old law book except some musty lawyers?"

She smiled and said, "You would be surprised."

My best friend from law school, Nancy K. McCarthy, concurred and suggested that we finally surrender to technology and purchase a legal research service. Things cascaded from there and well, here we are.

In the writing of this book, I had an unprecedented amount of assistance and support. From the Pagan world, I need to thank and acknowledge the following people: my contacts at The Witches' Voice, which is an amazing resource for Pagans; Dr. David L. Oringderff of the Sacred Well Congregation who contributed significantly regarding the sections devoted to Paganism and the military; Lieutenant Colonel Ron Schaefer graciously gave me an interview for this book; Tom Dixon (Walking Stick) and Rose Wise of Ozark Avalon unflinchingly shared the travails and triumphs of Ozark Avalon; Mr. Ron Koester in Ohio provided the information regarding the May, 2001 ritual of the Spirit Weaver's Church, one of the true life tales told in Chapter 7; and Nancy K. McCarthy who arranged the legal research service and always believed in me.

From my other support networks, I need to thank and acknowledge the following people. As always, this book would not be possible without the generosity and resources provided by my mother and father. My sister gave me her unconditional support and confidence. Attorney Craig Redler of St. Louis, Missouri, provided assistance in drafting some crucial language on some rather short notice, to say nothing of rendering his invaluable assistance in other areas. Ned Sonntag, who illustrated *The Practical Pagan*, tracked down quotes and references for me. His talent transcends the drafting table. My research assistant Caryn Morris was sent by the Goddess. We spent many wintry hours in a law library looking up citations (always trust in the power of books) and reading drafts of chapters. Carolyn Lynch who was drafted at the last minute can rant to me any time! Tim Coleman remains, as always, my invaluable right arm, and Michelle Neubauer provided a great deal of encouragement even after reading some of the rough material. To everyone on the e-mail lists who offered and shared information, thank you for your trust and for your support. I also had the support and assistance of the people in my office.

After graduating from law school cum laude in 1981, I was a lawyer in private legal practice from 1982 until 1998 in the states of Illinois and Missouri. During that time, I was ensconced in a legal community that showed no prejudice regarding my religious affiliations. The bench and bar in the great state of Missouri cared for one thing only: My competence as an attorney. My good fortune in this area continues to the present day as the people I work with have been nothing but understanding and supportive. Without the effort and support put forth by all these people, this book would never have been written.

CONTENTS

INTRODUCTION

Modern Paganism is a collection of spiritual traditions and paths, which, in other times, we might have called religions. However, most modern Pagans are recalcitrant regarding the use of the word "religion." Typically, Pagans refer to their personal set of beliefs and practices as a spiritual tradition or a spiritual path. Whatever they are called, as Pagans continue to insist that they are embracing legitimate spiritual paths, it is inevitable that Pagans will experience legal challenges. In the late 1990s, I observed that this was, indeed, occurring. At that time, people began posting to numerous lists and

Websites with problems: *I am being harassed at work because I am Pagan; I got fired because I am Pagan; I am being evicted because I am Pagan; they are going to take my kids away because I am Pagan; my husband is using Witchcraft against me in my divorce; the police came in my house and took my books and my candles, etc.* The Pagan folk were justifiably frightened. As my interaction with Pagans in these situations progressed, I learned that they were not well acquainted with the status of the law, how the law works, or with their rights in general.

This book responds to that growing crisis. In these pages, I hope to convey to Pagans a minimum understanding of the law and how it works. However, a single book does not a lawyer make; so, no one should use this book as an alternative to competent legal counsel obtained from within their communities. This book does not purport to take the place of competent legal counsel. No one should rely on this book as legal advice for how to behave in a certain situation. The only real answer is to get a lawyer.

Great, you are thinking. *So, what can I use this book for?* Use it to educate yourself, your family, your friends, your school board, and others whom you perceive to be infringing your rights. Then, get yourself some solid legal help. When you find yourself in a lawyer's office complaining about your work supervisor, your spouse, your landlord, etc., you might want to give the lawyer a copy of the book. The attorney may need a starting point for research. It would be helpful if you could provide that starting point, and this book might just be it.

As Pagans courageously come out of hiding necessitated by persecution and discrimination, they will face legal challenges because they are different. Typically, non-mainstream people must fight for their right to be what they are and their right to be legally secure in what they are. People of diverse faiths have had their day in court. Now, Pagans must step up to the plate. In so doing, we are fortunate to have a wealth of legal precedent upon which to draw, and that precedent exists because other non-mainstream believers, or non-believers, have already blazed this trail. We are not alone.

In the year 2002, the Pagan Pride Project reported record-breaking attendance at its events. At Pagan Pride events held in the United States, Canada, the United Kingdom, Italy, Portugal, and Brazil, event coordinators reported final attendance for 2002 at 29,506, representing an increase of more than 12,000 people over year 2001 participants. This attendance occurred despite the largest number of protestor incidents in Pride history, with protestors or observers being noted at several events, including Raleigh, NC; Dover, DE; Jackson, MI; Pittsburgh, PA; Winnipeg; Rochester, NY; and Dallas, TX. A new single event record was also set, with attendance at Jacksonville, Florida, Pagan Pride being conservatively estimated at 3,000. Brisbane, Australia, also reported attendance of approximately 2,000, as did Sacramento, California. (From Pagan Pride Project Press Release, October 14, 2002, Cecylyna Dewr, Executive Director, Pagan Pride Project.)

History teaches us that mixing religion and government is a patently bad idea. The United States Constitution and its first Ten Amendments, known as the Bill of Rights, is a watershed event in that history. Our form of government separates itself from religion and yet, we remain a deeply religious people. This is the great promise of the Constitution and the times in which we live. For the first time in history, a population widely diverse in its religious beliefs may live in a society without fear. This does not come without some sacrifice, as any person of color will tell you. Rights may be guaranteed, in theory, but they may also be denied in practice. Sometimes, you have to endure great unpleasantness and make certain sacrifices to safely hold those rights. This is not exactly fair, but it is a fact, as many of the litigants in the cases discussed in this book have discovered. Still, if our Pagan children are to be secure in their spirituality, then we of the previous generations must be prepared to clear the path so that they can forge ahead.

CHAPTER 1

PAGANS AND
THEIR LAWYERS

INTRODUCTION

As you will see in the following chapters, the court system was not created for laypeople. Figuring out what court you are in might be tough enough, but figuring out how to proceed can also be quite difficult, and you have not even gotten to the substance of your legal matter: that is, to the actual meat and potatoes law of why you are in court. Even if you are savvy enough to have gotten to the right place on the right kind of pleading, representing yourself *pro se* can become a weighty challenge, and to be frank, many judges are not that tolerant of *pro se* parties. If you are in danger of losing your children, a significant amount of cash, your home, your job, or anything else that you place great value on, you are probably going to need a lawyer.

There is no Pagan network of free Pagan lawyers

I have been on the Internet since the late 1990s working with several Pagan groups. I have yet to find an established network of Pagan lawyers who are in active practice and willing to take cases for free. There is no master list of practicing lawyers in the 50 states who are Pagan. Attempts have been made to create one, but to date those efforts have not been successful. There is no list of practicing lawyers in the 50 states that are both Pagan and who are willing to take your case for free.

Furthermore, if you are lucky enough to find a Pagan lawyer on the Net or anywhere else and ask them for advice on your case, it might be difficult to get that advice because some legal malpractice carriers really frown on this sort of thing. Hence, lawyers may be rather reluctant to dispense free legal advice on the Internet or in an e-mail. You might be fortunate enough to get some rather broad statements of the law, and then the person you are corresponding with will probably say, "You need to find a lawyer and raise these matters with her/him." Additionally, there are dangers related to protecting client confidentiality through the use of e-mail as a form of communication between lawyer and client. The danger of e-mail interception prompted the Missouri Bar Association at one time to issue a warning regarding e-mail as a form of client communication. At one time, the warning was located at *www.pw1.netcom.com/ ~jrossgood/warning.htm*

However, I was aware of one list whose members were mostly Pagan legal professionals: The Pagan Bar Association. At one time, they were located at *www.groups.msn.com/PaganBarAssociation.* There, matters were discussed among the members in a scholarly manner, and then some networking usually occurred in an attempt to find a needy party a lawyer. A lawyer might not necessarily be Pagan, but that is fine. What is important is that the lawyer is competent, local to you and to the legal venue you will be in, and has some expertise in the matters that concern you.

Additionally, there are some legal professionals who, from time to time, discuss current events and share their thoughts with AREN (Alternative Religious Education Network). The posting of a request for assistance or of information regarding a certain set of circumstances to the AREN Website *(www.aren.org/)* will probably find its way to that list. Once a situation is made known to this list, the list members discuss the matter amongst themselves in a scholarly manner, and may be able to network such that a referral to an attorney is made. Most Pagan legal professionals are willing to share any expertise they have with attorneys who contact them for help; for example, supplying resource and reference material such as reading lists, helpful Websites, case law, and the names of potential expert witnesses.

Usually, when I get a plea for a Pagan lawyer, I find out what state, town, or county the inquiring person is located in. Then, I go to one of several groups that I work with and put out a call for a lawyer in that area to contact the inquiring person. More often than not, there are just not enough openly Pagan lawyers networked into the Pagan community to satisfy the need for representation that exists. Even if a lawyer is found in the same state as the inquiring person, that lawyer may not be able to help the inquiring person. The lawyer may not be sufficiently proficient in the specific area of law that the inquiring

If you are looking for free legal advice or a low cost attorney, just enter the search terms "*pro bono* legal assistance" into your search engine. You will pull up dozens of Websites directing you to low cost legal assistance. Check with your state's bar association, usually located in your state's capital, for *pro bono* groups of lawyers or referrals to *pro bono* lawyers. There is a Website, *www.law.freeadvice.com/re-sources/linkbar.htm,* which references most, if not all, bar associations in the country.

person is dealing with, or the lawyer may not be close enough geographically to do the inquiring person any real good. For example, an attorney in Chicago, Illinois, may not be of much help to a potential party down in Mount Vernon, Illinois. Illinois is a big state, and it simply is not cost-effective for a Chicago lawyer to drive the six or seven hours it takes to get to Mount Vernon for court appearances and discovery matters such as depositions. Even if you are fortunate enough to procure the services of a lawyer who is a Pagan, do not assume that those services will come for free. Pagan lawyers went to law school and incurred huge debts in order to get through school. They have homes, families, and other financial obligations just like everyone else does. They will probably charge a fee of some kind for their services.

WHAT YOU WANT IS A GOOD LAWYER, EVEN IF HE OR SHE IS NOT PAGAN

Having a lawyer who is not a Pagan is not necessarily a bad thing. What you want is a good lawyer. You want someone who has experience in the type of case you have: a constitutional law case, a criminal case, an employment discrimination case, a child custody case, etc. You want a lawyer who is reasonably close to the court that your case is situated in so that you do not have to pay travel expenses. You want a lawyer who has previously practiced before this particular judge

The computer has really changed everything, and this is evident when seeking out attorney referrals. Each state has a bar association, usually located in the state capital. Many bar associations have Websites that are easily accessed. Simple searches on Web browsers that list the name of your state and a request for the bar association will yield fruitful results. You could start with *www.getareferral.com, www.law.freeadvice.com/resources/linkbar.htm,* or *www.lawline.org/lawclinics/missouri/legalaid-legaladvice.htm.*

or a lawyer who comes from a firm with other lawyers who have practiced before this particular judge in the past. You want a lawyer who is willing to talk to you like a human being, to do the research necessary to become familiar with your type of Paganism and your case, and who will be willing to handle the appeal, if necessary. If you find yourself in a legal situation such as a child custody matter, eviction proceedings, divorce proceedings, a landlord/tenant dispute, or criminal action, then it is critical that you seek the legal advice of a competent attorney within your community.

If you are worried about your attorney's credentials, check with the Martindale-Hubbell volumes for your attorney's listing, which can usually be found in any law library. So, while you are at the law library in the courthouse of your county seat, ask the librarian for the location of these volumes. They are organized by state. It may be worthwhile to take the time to look through the hard copy of the Martindale-Hubbell volumes. It is easier to find what you are looking for this way. Most attorneys and their credentials will be listed there. In addition to the huge volumes listing lawyers nationally, Martindale-Hubbell now has a Website with a lawyer locator feature. They can be found on the Internet at *www.martindale.com/*. On that Website, lawyers can be located by state and town. From there, they can be located by name and by specialty. Most attorneys will also have their law school degrees and state license accreditations hanging on the walls of their offices. If they are admitted to practice in specific courts, such as federal district courts or federal appellate courts, those licenses will probably be hanging on the walls of the office as well. If you are concerned about their professional ethics, check with the state bar association to see if there are any complaints lodged against your attorney for ethics violations.

Via phone, you can get the number for the state capital, and then you can ask for the State Bar Association. Dial the number. Inform whomever answers that you are looking for the bar association referral line. Once you have dialed that number and have gotten someone on the phone, tell them that you need an attorney in your particular county and your particular town whose expertise is in domestic issues, civil rights issues, etc. Very briefly explain what your problem is. You will probably receive a list of names or another source of information. You have to work from there.

I HAVE NEVER DONE THIS BEFORE!
WHAT DO I DO?

Once you have a list of names and telephone numbers, make the phone calls. Let's assume that your particular problem is child custody and your ex wants to take the kids away because you are a Druid. Advise the receptionist that you have a child custody problem and that you believe religion will be a major issue in your case. Tell the receptionist that you wish to speak to an attorney in that particular office with expertise in child custody and that you were referred by the state and/or local bar association. If you were referred by someone else, you will want to mention that person. Referral sources are important to attorneys.

Once you have the attorney on the line, do not launch into a historical account of events. Do not launch into a long recitation of your religious beliefs and a pile of complaints about how discriminated against you are. Simply say that you have a matter involving child custody and that religion will be an issue because you are not a member of a mainstream religion. Advise the attorney that you would like to meet for a consultation.

Effective communication with lawyers is a big issue. Most people are in a state of panic when they call lawyers. They don't know how to identify themselves properly on the phone, let alone coherently discuss their problem. I recommend that when you call, you identify yourself by name, by the town and county that you live in, and that you tell the office you are calling that you believe you may have a discrimination matter involving housing, employment, child custody, or whatever the case may be. For example, your opening salvo on the phone might sound like this: "Hello, my name is Joe Druid, and I live in the town of Celtria. I believe that I have an employment discrimination issue as I am being repeatedly harassed by my coworkers at work. I have informed my supervisor, but he is not doing anything. If your firm handles employment discrimination, I was wondering if I might come in for a consultation."

At this point, the attorney will probably ask you some questions involving your case, and she/he will probably ask you about your religion. At this stage in the game, it is critical that you are coherent about what you believe. For example, if the attorney asks you what a Druid is, you should be able to respond briefly, succinctly, and in a manner that sounds as benign as possible. For example, you might say: "A Druid is a person who practices a pre-Roman and pre-Christian form of Celtic religion that has been revived in the modern age. I belong to The Order of Bards, Ovates, and Druids, which is a society with roots in the Ancient Druid Order that was founded in 1717 C.E. in England. My religious beliefs are sincere, and I have practiced this spirituality for X number of years. I can provide you with a reading list, Websites, and other source material regarding my spirituality." Advise he or she that you need an advocate who will proactively assert your position and your rights, and who is willing to educate themselves regarding your non-mainstream religion.

As an attorney, I can tell you that no attorney likes to be the last person to find something out. We want to be the first to know, and if there is a potential problem or trouble spot with a case, we want to know immediately. Therefore, the best thing for you to do is to advise any attorney with whom you are dealing that you believe you have a potential discrimination problem, that the discrimination is related to religion, and that you belong to a Pagan religion such as Wicca, the Asatrú, Druidry, and all the rest. However, you do not want to overwhelm the lawyer or sound like you have a few pentacles loose.

At this point, the attorney will probably make a decision about whether they will even interview you in the office. If the attorney agrees to see you, ask if the consultation is free. Also, make the necessary inquiries about the fees. Is there an up-front fee? Does the attorney charge by the hour? What is that charge? Will the attorney take the case on a contingent basis? If the costs are prohibitive, then ask the attorney for another reference. Ask whether he/she can recommend you to anyone in particular.

Getting the ACLU to represent you might be harder than you think

The ACLU (American Civil Liberties Union) involves itself in civil rights cases, and if they take your case, their representation is usually free. So, how do they get paid? As part of their case, they usually demand that the opposing party pay their fees. The ACLU was instrumental in the Crystal Seifferly case, which involved an honor roll high school student who sued the local school board over her right to wear her pentacle in school. The ACLU represented her and in the negotiated settlement, the Defendant school board paid over $14,000 in legal fees to the ACLU.[1] You may wish to consider involving the American Civil Liberties Union in your case. Each state has an active ACLU branch. If one is located in your area, they can usually be found through the phone book or information in your area. If you have computer/Web access, the main ACLU site is *www.aclu.org*. From here, you can find all the ACLU offices in the country.

However, getting the ACLU to represent you is not as easy as you might think. Do not believe that the ACLU will take your case if you just call them up and tell them that you think you are the victim of religious discrimination. First, you will have to get someone to review your case, and it might take quite a bit of time just to get someone to call you back. If you have a matter that is time sensitive—that is, you have to do something before a certain date—you might not have enough time to involve the ACLU. Even if you are able to get an ACLU attorney to talk to you, you will have to convince them that you have a case of merit that is worth their time. They will probably have a form for you to fill out, and the form itself can be rather intimidating.

One Pagan organization tried to involve the ACLU in its legal matter and was not successful in getting the ACLU to represent them. In August of 2000, the Wiccan church of Ozark Avalon, located in Columbia, Missouri, was embroiled in a fight with the Tax Assessor of Cooper

County, Missouri. Having been declared a church and having been granted 501(c)(3) status by the IRS, Cooper County refused to grant Ozark Avalon a church-based tax exemption (discussed in detail in Chapter 7). Tom Dixon, the president of this not-for-profit Wiccan Church, contacted the ACLU and asked them for representation at the second stage of the administrative process, which was the state-level appeal board. Mr. Dixon's wait time for the ACLU was six weeks, and this put Ozark Avalon past the date set for the appeal. He also had to fill out a rather large and detail-intensive form that was required by the ACLU.

Even after having done all this, the ACLU declined to represent Ozark Avalon. Persons less tenacious than Tom Dixon and Rose Wise, the other Steward of Ozark Avalon, might have been discouraged and might have given up, but these two did not. Mercifully, Ozark Avalon found a local attorney who took their case, and Ozark Avalon was successful in obtaining its church-based tax exemption. A copy of the Missouri State Tax Commission's decision can be found on Ozark Avalon's Website.[2] It is a gold mine of legal references for Pagans and their lawyers.

There is one other organization specifically interested in the separation of church and state: Citizens for the Separation of Church and State. Their Website is located at *www.au.org/*. They are currently involved in the Cynthia Simpson case, which involves a Wiccan who wanted to be put on the list of clergy for performing opening invocation at meetings of the County Supervisors.[3]

THE LAWYER IS GOING TO THINK THAT I AM WEIRD

For most people, going to see a lawyer is about as much fun as a root canal. *The attorney is going to think that I am weird,* you are saying to yourself. *The attorney will never take my case.* But lawyers see a lot of weird people who somehow found themselves in very strange circumstances. Without weird people in very strange circumstances, most attorneys would not have jobs. So, relax! You are probably not the oddest apple in the barrel. Besides, there are ways to endear yourself to a lawyer right from the start.

When you go to see an attorney, be on time and keep your appointment. If you are married, your spouse should accompany you. Make arrangements for a babysitter if you have children. Take with you all court papers that you have, any and all documents pertaining to the legal matter (for example, if a landlord/tenant dispute, bring a copy of the lease, if you have one), and various resources regarding your spiritual tradition. Be ready and willing to educate your attorney on your particular religious tradition. This means that you must be educated and articulate regarding your religious/spiritual beliefs. You are the greatest singular resource your attorney has. Prepare a list of books, Websites, and other educational materials that will be beneficial to the attorney.

Additionally, you must go to the attorney's office with a good personal appearance. You should dress well, but casually. You do not need to wear a suit and tie or wear a dress with heels and stockings. However, your clothes should be clean and pressed. Keep jewelry and other bodily adornments at a minimum, and be assured of good personal hygiene. You should be freshly bathed with clean hair and well-barbered facial hair. An attorney is interested in a potential client who will make a good impression on either a judge or a jury. An unclean, unkempt appearance will almost certainly make a bad impression on the lawyer, and this could color her/his decision to take you as a client. The attorney will probably think that if you did not care enough to make a good impression in the law office, then you will not care enough to make a good impression to a judge or a jury. I have evaluated dozens of witnesses and clients during my years of litigation work, and in preparation for trial I have given this same speech to many of them. The ultimate goal here, in the mind of counsel, is to convince the trier of fact (whether a jury, an administrative agency, or a judge) that you, the client, are really no different from anyone else and that you want the same rights as anyone else.

By now, the attorney should realize that you are not a crackpot and that you are capable of making a good appearance in court, of giving credible testimony, and of being a great help in the preparation of your case. Lawyers like this sort of client. Now, there are some other items that you must discuss with the lawyer.

DISCUSSING FEES

On the issue of fees, be frank and candid with the attorney. Ask whether the attorney will require a retainer and if so, how much. Ask whether the file will be billed hourly and if so, what the hourly fee is. Inquire regarding costs and expenses, which are usually over and above the hourly fee. For example, there is a filing fee for the filing of a Petition and fees to be made to a process server for the service of process. Expert witnesses are usually paid hourly, and if depositions are taken, there will be fees to the court reporter. These are the sorts of fees that you may have to pay in addition to the cost of the lawyer.

Ask the lawyer if this is the sort of case that is taken on a contingency basis; that is, if the attorney will take a portion of a settlement or a judgment, once the settlement or judgment is rendered. A contingent case will require a defendant with assets, cash, or an insurance policy that covers litigation as part of the benefits to the policy. If there is no such Defendant, then this will probably be a case that is billed hourly, meaning that you will have to pay everything.

Even if a case is taken on a contingency basis, the attorney may still require that costs and expenses be paid by the client, even if the case is lost. Some attorneys may ask for a certain amount of money "up front" to cover initial expenses, even if a case is essentially a contingency case.

HOW AM I GOING TO PAY FOR THIS?

There is a running "joke" in the Pagan community, which states that Pagans are perennially poor and impecunious; they are not financially secure and have no real assets. For everyday, ordinary people who struggle with bills and financial obligations, this is not so very funny. Whether Pagan or not, most people do not have a couple of thousand dollars lying around to give to a lawyer to represent them. The last thing in the world anyone needs is to be involved in a lawsuit of some sort.

There are Pagans who have gone to their communities for money to finance a lawsuit. There are Pagans who have gone to more financially stable relatives and friends to finance lawsuits. You may wish to consider these options. Depending on the nature of the legal matter and how much it means to you, you may want to discuss the consequences of not contesting the matter with the lawyer. For example, if you work for an employer who gives you constant grief over your pentacle and if it is a job waiting tables at a lunch counter, you may wish to consider the option of finding another job rather than appearing before the EEOC. However, if you are faced with the prospect of losing your children to an ex-spouse whom you know to be abusive, then you may have to consider a number of options for financing, such as asking relatives or friends or going to your community. In some communities there are programs that you can join for a monthly fee, which will entitle you to legal assistance from that program for a multitude of legal situations. One such program operates out of St. Louis, Missouri, called the U.S. Legal Access Plan.

Talk with the lawyer about some creative billing. After the retainer, how often will you be billed? Can you set up a payment system? It may be that the attorney will be willing to work with you. You will never know unless you ask. This is no time to be shy or reticent. You must be your own advocate. However, do not ask the attorney to loan you money or front you money until your case is resolved. This is one way to lose a lawyer fast.

They took my case. Now what?

Remember that a lawyer provides you with a service. You are entitled to regular reports and phone calls from your attorney to see how the case is going once the attorney takes it. I highly recommend that you tell the attorney that you wish to receive a monthly progress report in writing regarding your case. Do not necessarily assume that "no news is good news." Good attorneys have dozens of cases because there are dozens of clients who want the good service that a good attorney provides. You are not the only person the attorney represents, but you want to be one of the most informed people that the attorney represents.

If you do not receive your first monthly progress report, call the office and request it. An attorney who is skilled in servicing their client will promptly return the phone call within a day or two. If you do not receive a return phone call, then call the attorney and ask to speak to his/her secretary or request that your message go in the attorney's voice mail. If you begin to feel that the attorney is trying to "dodge" you, then make an appointment with the attorney's secretary for a personal visit. It is much harder to explain away inappropriate representation in person than it is to do so on the phone.

After you receive your monthly progress report, review it immediately. Telephone your lawyer and advise them that you have received it. Ask questions, make comments, and make an appointment to see your attorney if you feel it is necessary. If your case has been taken on a contingent basis, then all this contact with the attorney is not costing you anything. However, if your case has been taken on an hourly billing basis, then every contact that you have with the attorney will cost you money, which the attorney will eventually bill you for. Time is money, after all.

Cooperate with your attorney. Failure to cooperate and follow your attorney's advice will give the attorney a legal basis for asking the judge to relieve him/her from the burden of representing you. In small communities, news that a client is difficult travels fast, and you might encounter some difficulty in finding a new attorney to represent you. Return telephone calls made by your attorney promptly. Review and respond to correspondence from your attorney promptly. Make yourself available for meetings, conferences, and depositions. Provide the documents that the attorney requests. Engage in meaningful conversations with your attorney, but try not to be argumentative or combative with them. This is your legal advocate, after all.

Many clients do not understand why an attorney needs so much information. This is simple: The rules regarding the discovery of information in the pre-trial phase of litigation are very liberal. For example, under the Federal Rules of Civil Procedure (discussed in Chapter 2), information need only be relevant to the subject matter of the case, and even though the information might not be admissible at trial, it could still be discoverable. Although your attorney might not think that certain information is relevant, opposing counsel might think that it is and make a request for it. An attorney cannot ignore a request for information. A response to the request must be made: either the information must be produced or your attorney may object to its discovery. If an objection is filed, the judge usually settles the dispute. However, it will be necessary for your attorney to see the documents or information requested *before* she/he produces them. No attorney wants to be the last person to know about information pertinent to their case. The last place they want to hear something for the first time is in court.

Your relationship with your attorney is confidential. Your conversations and communications with your lawyer are confidential. Her advice to you is confidential. This means that no one other than your lawyer and you are entitled to know what transpires between you. However, you could waive this privilege by talking about it, by posting it to e-mail lists, by putting it in press releases, or by posting it on Websites. Most attorneys will ask that you not discuss your case with anyone else. Talk with your attorney about whether you are at liberty to disclose details of your case, your court proceedings, etc. There have been Pagans who have been very public about their court proceedings. This could potentially backfire. Remember that once you have posted your life to a Website, it becomes a matter of public domain.

I MADE A MISTAKE HIRING THIS PAPER GLADIATOR, AND NOW I WANT A NEW ONE

Your attorney should work your case vigorously from start to finish. The monthly progress report should contain a discussion of the aggressive steps that the attorney is taking in representing you. It is your job to see to it that the attorney represents you in the manner you desire. It is possible to fire your attorney. If you are dissatisfied with the service you are receiving, you may obtain other legal counsel. However, you must first fire your current attorney.

First, you should go to see the attorney and advise them that you are unhappy with their service and wish to procure other counsel. Give the attorney a letter with a date on it which states that you are firing her/him effective as of the date of the letter, that you will be seeking other counsel, and that you are requesting a copy of your file. Get a copy of your file. Then, you must find other legal counsel. A new attorney cannot act on your case until you have fired your old attorney. Firing legal counsel is not a step to be taken lightly or for arbitrary and capricious reasons. Again, news that a client is difficult travels rapidly through a legal community, and if you acquire such a reputation, you may encounter some problems in procuring new legal counsel.

How did you get into this mess in the first place?

As this book should make abundantly clear, becoming involved in a legal matter could have far-reaching effects and will, most certainly, have a significant impact on your life. Other than money and the possible loss of child custody, a home, or a job, there is the daily stress of living with a legal situation. There is also the potential publicity that such a thing engenders. That publicity could affect not only you and your family, but it could affect your attorney as well. Some folks are able to handle living in this kind of fishbowl, while others are not. Publicity, which may at first seem welcome and helpful, can potentially backfire. Additionally, your case may conclude, and you might think that this is the end of it. However, your case could continue to be news and could continue to be important long after it is resolved, as a book like this demonstrates. Your name and your situation are going to be out there for a long, long time.

So, before you do the thing that is potentially going to land you in a lawyer's office, you may wish to take a step back and ask yourself: "Is it worth it?" Think hard on this. As some of the cases discussed in this book demonstrate, it takes a tremendous amount of courage, personal resolve, and resources to go public, to make a stand, and to fight for what you believe in. Weigh your options carefully and be candid with yourself.

CHAPTER 2

PAGANS AND THE AMERICAN COURT SYSTEM

INTRODUCTION

I t is important for everyone, not just Pagans, to know how the courts are organized, the theory under which matters are tried, and how to identify a matter once it is in the court. The federal courts are managed by the United States government, and these courts hear matters pertaining to federal law. You know the old saying: "Don't make a federal case out of it." The federal laws are codified in the United States Code, also known as the U.S.C. The annotated version of the United States Code is the U.S.C.A. (United States Code Annotated). The U.S.C.A. is a collection of books containing the federal laws and the cases decided according

to it. These items can be found in any law library. You
should be able to find a complete set of them at the law
library in the courthouse of your county seat.

For those of you who are wondering, your "county seat" refers to the
location of your county government. It is where your county courthouse
can be found, together with the county law library and other county
offices and agencies. Don't know where your county seat is? Most, if not
all, county and state offices can be accessed through the Web. A great
starting point for cross-referencing this information is *www.piperinfo.com/
state/index.cfm.*

Now then, the federal statutes can be found at Websites such as Lexis
and Westlaw, both of which are subscription services. You must pay
monthly fees to access these sites, although it may be possible to do brief
stints of research on them using your credit card. The federal statutes can
be accessed online free of charge through the Cornell Law School's Legal
Information Institute, and the main page is at *www.law.cornell.edu/.* The
page for the statutes is located at *www.law.cornell.edu/uscode/.*

THE FEDERAL COURT SYSTEM

The federal court system is comprised of the United States Supreme
Court, the federal district courts, the federal appellate courts, the U.S.
Court of Appeals for the Armed Forces, and certain courts with special
jurisdiction. These include the Tax Court, the Court of International
Trade, the Court of Veterans Appeals, and the Court of Federal Claims.
Online, there are some very good Websites for researching the federal
judiciary. You can begin with two of them: *www.uscourts.gov/* and
www.law.emory.edu/FEDCTS/.

The United States Supreme Court is located in Washington, D.C.,
and it is the supreme court of the land; hence, its name. The nine judges
who sit on the United States Supreme Court (fondly known as The
Supremes by many lawyers) are known as Justices. They are nominated

by the president, with the advice and consent of the United States Senate. Once seated, they hold their position for the duration of their lives, until they retire, or until they are removed from office. One of the nine Justices is the Chief Justice, and the others are Associate Justices. The United States Supreme Court hears cases arising out of the various state supreme courts and out of the federal appellate courts. It will also hear other cases over which it has specified jurisdiction.

The United States Supreme Court may refuse to hear certain cases. Filing an appeal with The Supremes does not necessarily mean that the case will be heard and decided by them. For example, the Missouri State Supreme Court case involving the Church of Scientology and that court's insistence that "religion" be defined by reference to a Supreme Being, was appealed to the United States Supreme Court, but the Justices found a reason to refuse to hear the case. It was dismissed summarily for want of federal question jurisdiction.[1]

The federal appellate courts are also known as the Circuit Courts. There are 12 Circuit Courts that encompass specified geographical areas; usually, at least three states apiece. For example, the Seventh Circuit Court of Appeals has jurisdiction over appellate matters arising out of the federal district courts for the states of Illinois, Indiana, and Wisconsin. The Eighth Circuit Court of Appeals has jurisdiction over appellate matters arising out of the federal district courts for the states of Arkansas, Iowa, Missouri, Nebraska, North Dakota, and South Dakota. The Circuit Court for the District of Columbia has jurisdiction over appeals arising out of the District of Columbia.

The U.S. Court of Appeals is a special appellate court that hears matters arising out of specified federal courts and federal agencies including, but not limited to, the International Trade Commission, the U.S. Court of Federal Claims, and the U.S. Court of Veterans Appeals. The judges who sit in the federal appellate courts are appointed for life by the president with the consent of the Senate. The federal appellate courts are comprised of at least six judges per the Circuit Court.

Lawyers who wish to practice before a particular federal appellate court must first be sworn before that court. Being sworn to practice in the

Eighth Circuit Court of Appeals is not a guarantee that the same lawyer can practice before the Seventh Circuit Court of Appeals.

The federal district courts are the courts of civil and criminal jurisdiction. These are where the federal trials are held. They are courts of general trial jurisdiction; that is, they have the power to hear most federal trial matters. The federal district courts have jurisdiction over cases arising under specified federal statutes, over civil and criminal cases, and over cases involving diversity subject matter jurisdiction. What is that? This usually means that the Plaintiff and the Defendant are residents of different states and that the amount of money involved is $75,000, exclusive of interest and costs.[2]

Federal district courts can be found in the Commonwealth of Puerto Rico, the U.S. Virgin Islands, the territories of Guam, the District of Columbia, the Northern Mariana Islands, and all 50 states. There are 94 district courts. Each district court has a bankruptcy unit that hears bankruptcy matters. Federal district judges are appointed for life by the president with the consent of the Senate.

The federal civil courts use a uniform system of evidence known as the Federal Rules of Evidence and a uniform system of civil procedure known as the Federal Rules of Civil Procedure. This collection of rules means that with minor exceptions, litigation is handled the same way in the federal courts whether that court is located in Massachusetts or Missouri. These rules are published yearly in soft-cover editions and can be found in the law library of your county seat and usually in other law libraries. Online, you can find the Federal Rules of Evidence at *www.law.cornell.edu/rules/fre/overview.html.* The site for the Federal Rules of Civil Procedure is located at *www.law.cornell.edu.rules/frcp/overview.html.*

Finally, each federal court will probably have local rules which it uses and which governs certain matters. Copies of a court's local rules can usually be obtained from the court clerk of that court. So, when appearing in the federal court, you need to be concerned not only with the substantive law, but with the procedural law as defined by the Federal

Rules of Civil Procedure and the local rules, together with the Federal Rules of Evidence.

THE STATE COURTS

The state courts hear matters pertaining to state law. These laws vary from state to state, and they are codified differently in every state. A copy of the codified state laws for all the states can be found in most law libraries, and they should be available in the law library in the courthouse of your county seat. If you are looking for a complete set of your state statutes, this is where you are most likely to find them, short of going to a law school library. Online, you can access your state statutes through the Cornell Law Schools' Legal Information Institute. The specific page is *www.law.cornell.edu/states/listing.html.*

The courts of the individual states are generally comprised of a state supreme court, state appellate courts, and lower state courts such as Probate Courts, Domestic Courts, and trial courts with both civil and criminal jurisdiction. Within the state courts, the trial courts of civil and criminal jurisdiction, together with the domestic and probate courts, are generally located in the city/town that is the county seat of any given county. For example, in the state of Missouri, there are 45 judicial circuits, and with the exception of the 22nd Circuit Court located in the City of St. Louis, all the judicial circuit courts are located in the County Seats of the Missouri Counties. If you wish to know which court your state case could be filed in, call the Circuit Court Clerk's office in your county and ask.

States usually have small claims courts where matters not in excess of a certain dollar amount can be tried without lawyers in a very simple manner. The small claims courts are user friendly; that is, they exist so that laypeople can resolve simple disputes in them without the services of lawyers. There are still rules that are going to apply, however. If you have a matter that can be tried in the small claims division of your state court system, it would be beneficial for you to actually go there and talk to the clerk of court for the small claims division. They probably have documents that outline the process for you.

When matters are appealed out of the trial courts, they are generally appealed to the state appellate courts. Some states have only one appellate court while other states have several. Each state has a state supreme court that hears matters on appeal out of the state appellate courts. Whether judges in the state courts are elected or nominated by officials such as the governor depends on the state and the particular judgeship in question.

A word to the wise: The clerks who work for the court system—no matter what court system—are very powerful and very busy people. Always be polite to these folks. Polite phone calls usually end with the caller getting the information they are looking for. Rude phone calls will not avail the caller very much. If you go to see them in person, good manners and a good appearance are a must. The polite, well-groomed visitor will usually get what it is they seek. The rude, slovenly buffoon will end up sitting in the waiting room all day.

The rules of evidence and of procedure for each of the state courts are different. Although the Federal Rules of Evidence are the acknowledged blueprint for evidentiary rules, differences between the federal rules and the state rules exist. Your state's rules of evidence may or may not be compiled in a book volume at the library, but on the Web, a good starting point for researching them is the following Web page: *www.expertpages.com/state_rules_of_evidence.htm.* Your state's procedural rules will be compiled in book form and can be found at law libraries. Online, a good starting point for researching them is *www.ssnx.com/courtrules/.*

Some mention needs to be made regarding the methods by which individual judges handle the daily business within their courts. A judge's calendar of cases is known as the *docket.* Once a case is filed, it receives a docket number. Every piece of paper filed in the case will have a docket number, and the court clerk will stamp it with a filing date. If you are calling a court clerk requesting information for a specific case, it helps if you know the docket number; the matter can most readily be found by use of its docket number.

Judges have individual clerks and/or secretaries who schedule appointments for them and screen their phone calls. If, for some reason, you need to speak to or see a particular judge, it is the secretary and/or clerk who is going to make these arrangements for you. Again, it is quite important that you comport yourself well when dealing with these folks.

YOUR ROADMAP TO FINDING A CASE

The American courts are directly descended from the English common law system. The common law refers to law that is not codified into statute; thus, the common law refers to a series of precedents on various issues. The precedents are found in the discussions of the cases. The case discussions, together with their precedents (usually known as holdings or rulings) are available for public consumption in volumes known as reporters. References to the cases and the reporters who publish these cases are known as *citations*. For example, federal trial cases are reported in the Federal

If you are looking for a case in a law library, then the citation of the case is your roadmap to the location of that case in the library. For example, look at the following citation: *Joe Druid v. Lilly Fairy*, XX F. 2d yyy (8th Cir. 2001). In this theoretical case, Joe Druid is the Plaintiff, and Lilly Fairy is the Defendant. The case could be found in the second edition volume XX of the Federal Reporter at page yyy. It would be a year 2001 Eighth Circuit appellate case.

Supplement, published by West Law Publishing Company. Federal appellate cases are reported in the Federal Reporter, also published by the same company. These citations to the cases appear after the names of the cases, which are designated in terms of *Plaintiff v. Defendant*.

Your roadmap to finding a statute

A *statute* is a law passed by a legislative body. For example, the federal statutes are passed by Congress. State statutes are passed by the state congressional bodies. Federal and state statutes also appear in book volumes. One state may have several different sets of volumes that contain their statutes; another state may have only one volume set that contains

their statutes. Federal statutes, which are the codified laws of the United States government, are found in the United States Code (U.S.C.) and the United States Code Annotated (U.S.C.A.). A citation to either of these might read like this: 28 U.S.C.A. Sec. 1332. This refers to number 28 of the United States Code Annotated, Section 1332. The citation to the statute is your roadmap to the location of the statute in the law library. The statute can be found in the

When lawyers and judges write their opinions, briefs, motions, and legal memoranda, they make extensive use of citations to cases, statutes, etc. I will be doing the same thing in this book. A citation appearing after a section of text means that the author of the text is referring to the citation as supporting authority for the point which is being made. Reference the notes for the sources.

Westlaw volume contained number 28 of the United States Code Annotated, Section 1332.

What is true in one court is not necessarily true for the others

For most Pagans, the state courts and possibly the federal trial and appellate courts will be the courts of greatest concern. These are the courts that will hear constitutional issues, child custody matters, landlord problems, property cases, and many employment issues. If one court makes a particular ruling on a particular issue, then that one ruling is not necessarily binding on everyone else. The American court system does not function like the rings of power created by Sauron in the *Lord of the Rings* trilogy.

The state courts must follow the rulings from the United States Supreme Court. The federal district courts and the federal circuit courts must follow the rulings of the United States Supreme Court. Within a federal appellate circuit, the federal district courts must obey the rulings of the federal appellate circuit court wherein the particular federal district court is located. For example, the federal district court of the eastern district of Missouri must obey precedents established by the Eighth Circuit Court of Appeals.

However, if there is no mandate from the United States Supreme Court and no mandate from the federal appellate court within which a federal district court is located, the federal district courts are free to interpret cases and laws as they see fit. Thus, it is possible to have federal district courts within a specified appellate circuit in disagreement over the same issues.

Similarly, the federal appellate courts are free to disagree with one another in the absence of a mandate from the United States Supreme Court. Thus, it is possible for the federal appellate courts to disagree with one another on the same issues. For example, there is currently a dispute among the federal appellate courts regarding the Second Amendment to the Constitution and the right of citizens to bear arms.[3]

In some instances, federal courts rule on matters of state law. If the Eighth Circuit Court of Appeals is hearing a case involving Missouri law, then that court is obliged to follow Missouri law on the subject. However, a Missouri state court may choose to ignore a federal court's pronouncement on the same issue. It does not happen all that often, but it does happen.

The state trial courts are bound to follow the law of the state in which they sit. When cases are appealed out of the state trial courts, they go to state appellate courts. If there is no uniformity on the issues involved, it is possible for the various state appellate courts to disagree with one another on the same issue. A pronouncement from the state supreme court will end the inconsistency and provide the precedent which all the state courts must then follow. State laws vary widely from state to state. For example, the factors that a court may consider when granting custody of a child to a parent may differ significantly from state to state. This is why people involved in lawsuits or who are parties to litigation should obtain competent legal counsel within their communities.

Our court system is known
as an adversarial system

Finally, you need to understand that the American legal system is an adversarial system. The theory under which the American courts operate is one of adversaries fighting it out. Just as gladiators fought it out in the Colosseum at Rome, just as knights battled to determine who was right and who was wrong in Arthurian legend, so do opponents slug it out in American courts. In the adversarial system, lawyers are known as advocates. They are the representatives of their clients, and they assert what will win the case for their respective clients. Preparation is key. Without it, a client loses. That is how the adversarial system works.

In most matters, the advocates battle out their cases before a judge or a jury. In a case tried before a jury, the people sitting in the jury determine what is the truth and what is not the truth. In a jury-tried case, the facts are as the jury decides them to be. A jury may choose to believe or not believe a witness. That is what the jury is there for. For example, in our theoretical case of Joe Druid versus Lilly Fairy, if Plaintiff Joe Druid testifies to "X" and Defendant Lilly Fairy testifies to "Not X," the jury is free to believe either of them or neither of them.

In order to make your case to either a judge or a jury, you must have evidence. The party who brings the suit (the Plaintiff) has the burden of proof; that is, the Plaintiff must present sufficient evidence to prove his/ her case. Evidence that is not heard or which does not survive a challenge by opposing counsel does not count. From the Plaintiff's perspective, the Plaintiff presents sufficient evidence to meet the burden of proof, argues his/her case to the jury, and hopes for a Plaintiff's verdict. The Defendant refutes that proof and, if necessary, presents his/her own proof, argues his/her case to the jury, and hopes for a Defendant's verdict rather than a Plaintiff's verdict.

Like it or not, justice in the American system is pretty much what the jury says it is. If a case is tried before a judge without a jury, then it would be equally fair to say that justice is exactly what the judge says it is. If the case is overturned on appeal, then justice was what the appellate court said it was. Justice is pretty much a matter of proof expertly presented and expertly argued. It might not be fair, but that is the way it is, and I hope that we all realize how fortunate we are at this point in history to have the system we've got. Things were once a whole lot worse, as you'll see in the last chapter.

Now that you're in the right place, what's the process?

I am often asked: "Can they sue me for this?" The answer is that if someone is capable of drafting a well-framed Petition/Complaint, of paying the court costs for the initial filing, and of paying for service of the Petition/Complaint either through the sheriff's office or through a private process server, then anyone can be sued for anything. Whether the suit will be successful is another story.

The courts are literally choked with frivolous and stupid lawsuits. However, it is the Judge who decides whether a lawsuit is frivolous or meritorious of being heard. Frivolous cases are usually dismissed by the judge before they reach trial. The most common method for disposing of the lawsuit that is without merit is the Motion to Dismiss for Failure to State a Cause of Action. This is commonly known as the Rule 12(b)(6) motion from the Federal Rules of Civil Procedure. All states have a version of this. The rule essentially provides that even if what the Petition/Complaint alleges to be true is in fact true, there is no lawsuit because the facts do not present a situation under which any sort of recovery can be had. Even so, a person who is sued in a frivolous case must still incur the costs and stress of defending themself and of convincing the judge to dismiss the case. If you are served with a lawsuit, for example, you cannot simply say, "This is stupid," and throw away the summons. You will have to answer in some fashion within the time frame stated in the summons. The best way to respond is to find an attorney, give her the summons and the Petition/Complaint, and allow the attorney to file your Answer, together with the Rule 12(b)(6), or its equivalent. The attorney will have to research the law to provide the Memorandum of Law that supports the motion, prepare the Memorandum, and appear in court to argue the motion.

Court process, whether civil or criminal, is serious business. It is nothing like it is portrayed in either television or movies. This chapter will now follow a civil suit, not a criminal suit. If you are involved in a court matter, you should procure competent legal counsel within your community.

The commencement of the case

A civil case is usually about money, otherwise known as financial remuneration or financial damages. The Plaintiff is the party who hopes to get the money. The Defendant hopes not to pay any money. The Plaintiff must formulate a Petition or a Complaint, file the suit in the appropriate court, pay the filing fees, and also pay to have the Defendant served with the lawsuit. Depending on the state, the court, and the type of case involved, filing fees can be negligible or they can be considerable. For example, in the state of Massachusetts, it costs $210 to file a civil case in the superior court. The fee to the sheriff for service on one defendant is $20.

The opening document of the case is the Petition/Complaint. It sets forth the various theories of legal action under which the Defendant will be held accountable. In legal parlance, that accountability is known as *liability*. So, each theory is known as a theory of liability. For example, a Defendant may be accountable/liable for trespass ("The Defendant trespassed on my property when he put up a sign in my front yard that said

'Witches go home.' "). That same action may render the Defendant liable under another statute ("That constitutes a hate crime under my city's ordinances.").

Once an individual has been served with process, they will have a specified amount of time within which to formulate some type of responsive pleading. You may have as little as 20 days. Check your state's rules. Parties to the suit, known as *litigants*, may choose to represent themselves, which is known as being *pro se*, or they may obtain legal representation. It is strongly suggested that you have competent legal counsel from within your community if you are either a Plaintiff or a Defendant. Parties who represent themselves *pro se* do not often procure the results that they desire and more often than not, *pro se* parties do not know what they are doing. This can be irritating to a judge with a busy docket.

Once you have been served with process, you have a finite number of days to respond. Failure to respond in a timely manner may result in a default judgment against you; this means that if you fail to respond or appear in court as ordered, the Plaintiff wins, regardless of the merits of their case. Check your state's Rules of Civil Procedure. Although default judgments can, in some instances, be set aside, it is not advisable for a Defendant to allow a default judgment to be taken against him or her. If you have been served with process, obtain competent legal advice immediately, but do not just sit there and hope that it will go away. It won't.

So, YOU WANT TO FILE A COUNTER SUIT

A common comment that I hear is: "I was wrongly sued, and I am going to file a counter suit." If a frivolous case was brought against you, and if it has been dismissed by the judge, you may have a case for malicious prosecution. Generally, the elements of a cause of action for malicious prosecution based on the previous underlying civil action are: the Defendant initiated a civil action against the Plaintiff; the civil action terminated in favor of the Plaintiff; the Defendant had no reasonable basis for bringing that civil action (put another way, that the Defendant had no probable cause for bringing that civil action); the Defendant brought the civil action with malice; and the Plaintiff suffered distinct economic harm as a result of that civil action.[4] Your state's case law and jury instructions should be researched for the specifics in your state, such as definitions of malice, probable cause, and economic harm.

However, suits for malicious prosecution are not favored under the law. Although you may file such a case, it is very difficult to bring such a case to successful conclusion.[5] The evidence required for success is usually very difficult. Please consult a competent attorney within your community if you think you would like to bring a case for malicious prosecution.

So, you received a Subpoena

A Subpoena is valid court process. If you receive a Subpoena, then you have received an official court command to appear at the specified time and place for a specified purpose. You do not have to be a party to a lawsuit to be served with a subpoena. Your presence could be required as a party to a law suit, as a witness to give a deposition, or as a witness to give testimony at trial. In any of these scenarios, you are being required to appear by the court that issued the Subpoena.

You are not at liberty to ignore a Subpoena. If you ignore a Subpoena, the judge has the power to dispatch a marshal or a sheriff to either your home or your place of employment and bring you before the court. In addition to giving testimony, you may face certain penalties for having ignored the Subpoena. You can be held in contempt of court by the judge.

If you must take time off from work to comply with the Subpoena, you will not necessarily receive financial recompense for missed time from work. Probably, you will not. Even if a state statute or rule of court provides for financial recompense, it will not be at a rate commensurate with your job.

So, YOU RECEIVED A SUMMONS FOR JURY DUTY

One of the responsibilities commensurate with voting and citizenship is jury duty. The names of all voters are on a roster somewhere in your county seat, and you are eventually going to receive a summons for jury duty.

You are not at liberty to ignore a call for jury duty. You must go, or be subject to certain penalties. A simple phone call is not going to get you off the hook. You must go to the courthouse as commanded and go through the process. You may or may not get out of jury duty, depending on how you answer the questions that the attorneys put to you when all the potential jurors are interviewed for a case.

Although most states provide for financial recompense for jury duty, it is usually in a very small amount, but usually it is not at all commensurate with the salaries of the potential jury members. Your employer must permit you to leave work for jury duty. So, if you have received a summons for this civil obligation, advise your employer immediately.

PREPARING EVIDENCE IN THE CIVIL CASE

In a civil matter, once the case is filed, the evidence must be collected. The process of gathering and preparing the evidence prior to trial is known as Discovery. Attorneys have various tools at their disposal during the Discovery process: Interrogatories, Request for Production of Documents, Depositions, and Request for Admission are the most commonly used methods of collecting information during Discovery. These are all covered under your state's Rules of Civil Procedure. Check the rules in your individual state.

If you are a party to a lawsuit, you will probably have to answer Interrogatories, which are written questions prepared by your opponent. When you receive your Interrogatories, whether you are a Plaintiff or a Defendant, understand that you have a limited amount of time within which to answer the Interrogatories and get them on file in the court. An extension of time can be obtained, and parties will usually obtain at least one extension. However, this extension may or may not be automatic. If it is not automatic, it must be applied for and granted by the judge, usually with the agreement of the other party.

Some of the questions asked in the Interrogatories may be objectionable, and you will not be required to answer them. However, objections must be raised before the judge, argued, and ruled upon. Do not automatically assume that just because you do not like a question or know that a similar question was thrown out of court in an episode of *L.A. Law* that you are not going to have to answer it. If you have a problem with any of the questions in the Interrogatories, raise your concerns with your attorney. If you are representing yourself, then you must understand that you are presumed to know the law and that it is also presumed that you will take the appropriate steps to make and to preserve whatever objections you have.

Another tool used in Discovery is known as the Request to Produce Documents. If you receive one of these, then you are being commanded to produce the items set forth in the request. Just as with the Interrogatories, some of the requests may be objectionable. If you have concerns about the requests, then raise those concerns with your attorney. Again, if you are representing yourself *pro se*, you are presumed to know what requests are or are not objectionable and will handle them accordingly.

A useful but expensive tool for discovery is the deposition. This is a recorded statement taken before a certified court reporter. The court reporter takes down everything that is said and transcribes the session into a booklet that reads like a play. This document is the deposition. Depositions are taken for two main purposes: to find out what a witness has to say, and to preserve that testimony so that it is available at trial in case a witness should die, go into a coma, or be otherwise unavailable for trial.

In some instances, the deposition can be read at trial, and the testimony in it will be heard just as if the witness had appeared live. In many instances, however, the deposition cannot be read at court and even though a witness has given a deposition, that witness will still have to appear at court to give live testimony. Once in court, the witness can be cross-examined using the deposition transcript. If court testimony contradicts deposition testimony, rigorous cross-examination will ensue in an attempt to determine why the witness' story has changed. Obviously, it is important to tell the truth from the beginning.

The court reporter that takes the deposition charges a fee. It must be paid. If an expert witness is giving a deposition, that expert witness is charging a fee for appearing and giving the testimony. That fee will have to be paid. Attorneys appearing for the deposition are probably charging by the hour, and they will have to be paid. This is expensive business.

Another useful tool for amassing evidence is the Request for Admissions. This is a written list of assertions that the opposing party will want to read to the jury as facts. Only parties to the lawsuit are obligated to answer a Request for Admissions. This tool is not used with mere witnesses. It is reserved for the parties. Some of the Requests for Admissions may be objectionable. If you receive a Request for Admissions, understand that if you say "Admitted" to any of them, then you have conceded that the point is true. That is why it is called an Admission. If you have any concerns about the Admissions, raise them with your attorney. If you are representing yourself, be very careful with these. You are expected to know the discovery law regarding the Request for Admissions and to take appropriate action.

WHAT HAPPENS AT TRIAL?

In my years as a Missouri civil litigator, I found that the members of the bench in the City of St. Louis and in the County of St. Louis were very aggressive in helping parties reach pre-trial solutions to their cases. In most civil cases, the judges called for pre-trial conferences in an attempt to effectuate some settlement to avoid incurring the time and expense of a trial. On the day a trial began, attorneys were usually before the judge in a pre-trial conference attempting to settle their cases and hearing pre-trial matters. Those pre-trial matters typically included Motions in Limine; that is, pre-trial motions designed to exclude certain evidence from the jury's domain. In the event that settlement cannot be reached, a trial commences.

Real-life trials look nothing like those you see on television programs or in the movies. The truth of the matter is that real-life trials can be very boring. They are governed by rules of evidence and of procedure. The better one knows these rules, the more masterful one is during the trial. Having mastery of these rules can mean the difference between getting crucial evidence in front of the jury or having it excluded. This can mean the difference between winning and losing. This is why it is best to have an attorney handling your trial.

A trial usually begins with the seating of a jury. The attorneys will determine who it is that they want to hear the case. There will be a question and answer session with the potential jurors, which is known as *voir dire*. At the end of *voir dire*, the jury will be seated. At that point, the attorneys usually engage in their opening statements. This is where they outline their respective theories of the case and the evidence that they will present to prove their theories. Because the Plaintiff has brought the suit and bears the initial burden of proof, the Plaintiff's attorney makes her opening statement first.

After the opening statements are made, the Plaintiff's counsel presents her case. For each theory of liability there will be specific elements to the cause of action, which must be proved. Failure to prove each element of each Cause of Action could result in a Motion for Directed Verdict, which means that the Plaintiff loses on that particular theory of liability. Proof in court can take the form of testimony from either live witnesses or from deposition transcripts that are read before the jury; answers to Interrogatories; admissions to a Request to Admit; or from physical evidence such as documents, photographs, videotapes, or other things that are put before the jury for its viewing. In medical malpractice cases, I have seen pathological slides be admitted into evidence, restraints, and laparotomy sponges. In product liability cases, I have seen mechanical items such as car parts admitted into evidence. However, a proper evidentiary foundation for all these items must be sufficiently made before they can be admitted into evidence.

A good attorney knows the answer to every question before it is asked, and most good trial attorneys will tell you that they never ask a question in trial to which they do not already know the answer. Defense counsel will have the opportunity to cross-examine all the witnesses that Plaintiff's counsel put on the stand. After the Plaintiff's case has been presented, defense counsel has its opportunity to present the case for the Defendant. The same sorts of evidence can be admitted. Plaintiff's counsel will have the opportunity to cross-examine all the witnesses that Plaintiff's counsel put on the stand.

During the trial, counsel will be making objections to various pieces of evidence being presented by their opponent. A ruling of "sustained" means that the objection has been sustained, and that piece of evidence has been removed from the case: It is not to be considered by the jury. A ruling of "overruled" or "denied" means that the objection has been denied: The piece of evidence is still in the case. If counsel is unhappy with an evidentiary ruling and wishes to preserve that ruling for appeal, counsel must make an offer of proof on that evidentiary ruling. That will probably mean a conference among the lawyers and the judge at the bench with the court reporter taking down all that occurs so that the record of these events is preserved for the appeal.

At the end of the presentation of all the evidence, both lawyers will usually make Motions for a Directed Verdict: They will ask the judge to rule on the evidence without putting it to the jury. Check your state's rules regarding Motions for a Directed Verdict. These motions are rarely granted, but lawyers must make them, nonetheless. Check your state's Rules of Civil Procedure for information about this particular motion. Now, closing arguments are made, and the matter is submitted to the jury.

When the judge submits the case to the jury, the judge presents the jury with instructions for the theories of liability presented by the Plaintiff and for the theories of defense presented by the Defendant. These are formal instructions that are usually set forth in a book of jury instructions. Because theories of liability can differ from state to state, each state will have its own compilation of approved jury instructions. An improperly submitted or formulated jury instruction can be a basis for appeal.

Once the jury has made its decision, the decision of the jury is read in open court, and the jury is dismissed. If the losing party is unhappy with the results, he/she may file a Motion for Judgment Notwithstanding the Verdict; however, this motion must be made within the time frame specified by the rules, and it can usually be made only if that party filed a Motion for Directed Verdict. Again, check your state's rules regarding filing a Motion for a Directed Verdict. The case is now ready for the appellate process.

WHAT HAPPENS AFTER TRIAL?

Once a verdict is returned, the losing party may wish to appeal the decision. There will be rules regarding the time limitations for filing a Notice of Appeal and all the supporting items that the appellate court will need to make a decision, usually the trial transcript, important pieces of pleading made throughout the case, and the evidentiary items that were before the jury. Failure to meet deadlines could result in loss of all appellate rights, which means that whether you think the jury decision was good or bad, you are stuck with it. In matters involving state law, cases can potentially be appealed all the way to the state supreme court.

Appeals are costly. The cost of a trial transcript, depending on the size of the transcript and the length of time it took to try the case, can be thousands of dollars. Then, you also have to pay the attorney to prepare, file, and argue the appeal. If you lose your appeal or if you decide not to appeal, then both parties may still engage in some useful settlement discussion, but usually the losing party must now pay the piper, so to speak. If monetary damages have been awarded, this means that the defendant must now pay up. In car accident cases, this is where the Defendant's auto liability insurer pays the amount specified by the jury to the Plaintiff. In cases for back child support, this is where the delinquent parent has to pay the money owed for support of the children which has, hitherto, gone unpaid. If the Defendant cannot pay up, the Plaintiff has several tools he may utilize, including the placement of a lien on real estate owned by the Defendant or garnishing the Defendant's wages.

If you want to see a real trial, check with the court clerk in your county seat and go watch one. Trial judges put their dockets in order on nearly every Monday of the year, and trial begins. It may take the mystery out of the process, but it will certainly convince you that a trial is not an episode of *L.A. Law*. Now you have some familiarity with the civil process, and you hopefully understand why having an attorney to represent you is a good idea.

CHAPTER 3

PAGANS AND THE FIRST AMENDMENT

"Congress shall make no law respecting an establishment of religion, or prohibiting the free exercise thereof; or abridging the freedom of speech, or of the press; or the right of the people peaceably to assemble, and to petition the Government for a redress of grievances."

—U.S. Const. Amend. I

INTRODUCTION

The Federal Constitution is a remarkable document that represents a defining moment in human history. In the First Amendment, religion and government are separated from one another, thus leaving the citizenry free of governmental involvement and constraints regarding individuals and their spirituality, or lack of it. Although a noble and ambitious undertaking, the struggle to firmly demarcate religion and government in court has been arduous, but by its nature peaceful. The body of law that represents this struggle is known as constitutional law because it addresses this fundamental underpinning of our society and our government. Thus, an understanding of how religion, government, and the Constitution have evolved is basic to understanding any other type of law that affects religion, such as employment law or housing law, and all the rest.

However, most people read the Constitution in the eighth grade and forgot about it. It is highly recommended that everyone read this document, boring as it appears. It is what stands between you and 10 thousand years of discrimination, persecution, and darkness. A copy of the Constitution should be on every citizen's bookshelf. A basic understanding of the Constitution, the First Amendment, and their history is essential to grasping the enormity of religious freedom. Although veritable libraries have been written on these topics, this chapter will address these issues in a manner that is specifically pertinent to Pagans.

A copy of the Constitution can be found in public libraries and in all law libraries. It can be found on the Internet by simply inserting the terms "United States Constitution" into your search engine. An annotated version can be found at *www.acess.gpo.gov*. You can also pick up *The Declaration of Independence and The Constitution of the United States, with an Introduction by Pauline Maier* (New York: Bantam Books, 1998).

To briefly summarize, the United States Constitution creates and empowers the three branches of the United States government: the executive branch (the presidency); the legislative branch (comprised of the United States Senate and House of Representatives); and the judiciary (the courts). Literally, the Constitution is the blueprint for the federal government, its powers, and its limitations. It also creates the judiciary, which has become the watchdog of the legislative branch and of the executive branch. The first 10 amendments are known collectively as the Bill of Rights, and it is the First Amendment that guarantees religious freedom. Any conversation regarding religious freedom must begin here.

The United States Supreme Court can invalidate acts of Congress by declaring them unconstitutional. For example, the United States Supreme Court declared the 1993 Religious Freedom Restoration Act unconstitutional. According to the Supreme Court, Congress acted beyond its constitutionally specified powers by enacting the legislation.[1]

THE FIRST AMENDMENT

The First Amendment famously begins: "Congress shall make no law respecting an establishment of religion, or prohibiting the free exercise thereof...." The body of case law interpreting this phrase is prodigious. However, as to religion, two distinct lines of cases arise under this clause: the Free Exercise clause cases and the Establishment of Religion clause cases. We will deal with these two different aspects of the amendment, together with their standards of review, later in this chapter. Hidden in this deceptively simple passage are some problems that are not readily apparent, even to the most careful reader.

To begin, the First Amendment as written applies only to the federal government. The federal government cannot establish religion in America or interfere with a citizen's free exercise of religion. The Federal Constitution and its amendments do not apply to or include the state governments. So, taken alone, the First Amendment is not applicable to state governments. However, by operation of the Fourteenth Amendment, the limitations of the First Amendment are imposed upon the legislative branches of the state governments and their political subdivisions. As blatant a problem as this seems to be, the issue of applying the First Amendment to actions taken by state governments was not fully addressed until the *Cantwell* decision in 1940, just over 60 years ago.[2]

Additionally, the amendment does not define "religion," a problem that was noted by the Supreme Court in 1878 when dealing with the tricky issue presented by the Mormon religious practice of polygamy in the Territory of Utah in the case *Reynolds v. United States* (98 U.S. 145 [1878]). At the time, the Mormon litigant believed he had a religious duty to keep multiple wives, which put him squarely at odds with a federal law preventing polygamy in the Territories. The Supreme Court did away with the conflict between individual religious practice and federal law quite simply: "Polygamy has always been odious

Mormonism, polygamy, and the assertion of religious freedom remain current topics. In 2003, the head of a polygamist sect publicly criticized a Senator who lumped polygamy together with such practices as incest, adultery, and homosexuality. To learn more, see the article "Sect Leader Objects to Santorum Comments," from *U.S. National Associated Press*, available online at *www.story.news.yahoo.com/news?tmp=story&ncid=519&e=50&u=/ap20030424.*

among the northern and western nations of Europe, and, until the establishment of the Mormon Church, was almost exclusively a feature of the life of Asiatic and of African people. At common law, the second marriage was always void...and from the earliest history of England polygamy has been treated as an offense against society."[3]

The difficult threshold issue thus becomes: what is religion? The second issue is: who defines religion? These are tricky matters with which both the courts and the legislature have wrestled with over the years. Although the notion of a third party defining our beliefs as religious may seem absurd or even offensive, it cannot be avoided when analyzing situations under the First Amendment because only beliefs that have their roots in religion will be afforded constitutional protection.[4]

DEFINING RELIGION

Both the courts and the legislature have defined "religion." The courts often perform this task as a preliminary issue in Free Exercise or Establishment cases. In these situations, the courts are called upon to determine whether practices/beliefs are religious in nature so as to merit First Amendment protection.

The courts are not particularly comfortable with this duty and have called it a "notoriously difficult, if not impossible task."[5] The difficult business of court-crafted definitions of religion has been ongoing since the *Reynolds* case in 1878, and numerous scholars have studied this conundrum in some depth.

Read Rebecca French's article, "From Yoder to Yoda: Models of Traditional, Modern, and Postmodern Religion in U.S. Constitutional Law," 41 ARIZ. L. REV. 49, (1999) at footnotes 11 and 12. Ms. French provides numerous references for studying this ongoing battle. The Second Circuit Court of Appeals has done a fair job of outlining this historical battle, as well. See also the *Krishna Consciousness* case, pages 439-440, and the footnotes therein.

When enacting laws on specific topics, legislatures often build definitions of religion into the statutes themselves. For example, the Religious Land Use and Institutionalized Persons Act, commonly known as the RLUIPA and codified at 42 U.S.C.A. sections 2000cc, *et seq.,* addresses land use regulation and the free exercise of religion without undue governmental interference. The statute defines a religious exercise in general: "The term 'religious exercise' includes any exercise of religion, whether or not compelled by, or central to, a system of religious belief."[6] What does this mean? At least one federal court has found that this simply means a sincerely held belief that is religious in nature.[7] The Civil Rights Act of 1964 also sets forth a definition of religion: "To be a bona fide religious belief entitled to protection under either the First Amendment or Title VII, a belief must be sincerely held, and within the believer's own scheme of things religious."[8]

A particularly fertile source of case law regarding legislative definitions of religion has arisen out of the military context. Known as *conscientious objector* cases, these decisions usually involve military inductees seeking to be absolved of military duty on the basis of their religious convictions. One federal statute at the heart of these quarrels has been the Universal Military Training and Service Act, Sec. 6J, as amended 50 U.S.C. Ap Sec. 456(j)(1948). Herein, Congress set forth the meaning of a religious belief: "...an individual's belief in a relation to a Supreme Being involving duties superior to those arising from any human relation but [not including] essentially political, sociological, or philosophical views or merely moral personal code." Arguably, the definitions of religion formulated by the Supreme Court in the conscientious objector cases are applicable only to these cases. As we shall see, however, the same language adopted by the Court in these cases keeps re-appearing in other places.

In the case of *United States v. Seeger* (380 U.S. 163 [1965]), the Supreme Court faced the daunting task of interpreting the Universal Military Training and Service Act. In this conscientious objector case, the initial problem was identifying the Supreme Being mentioned in the Act. The Court found itself asking: Could a conscientious objector believe only in an orthodox god or in something else? The Supreme Court

Historically, several cases are instructive on judicial definitions of religion because they have involved and led to the modern definitions seen in the statutes quoted previously. For example, in the case of *Wisconsin v. Yoder* (406 U.S. 205 [1972]), Amish parents did not wish to educate their children in public schools. In that case, the Court stated that "to have the protection of the Religion Clauses, the claims must be rooted in religious belief."[9] Admitting that determining what constitutes a religious belief or practice is a "most delicate question,"[10] the Court stated that philosophical or personal beliefs did not rise to the level of religious belief protected under the First Amendment and opined that "the very concept of order and liberty precludes allowing every person to make his own standards on matters of conduct in which society as a whole has important interests."[11] In this case, the Supreme Court found that the Amish were living lives of "deep religious connection,"[12] and that their way of life did not reflect mere personal preference.

Justices determined that religious belief could be founded not only in an orthodox god, but also in something else. In attempting to identify that something else, the Court asserted that a believer could have a relationship with a "power or being, or a faith, 'to which all else is subordinate or upon which all else is ultimately dependent.'"[13] However, a mere personal moral code would not pass muster. The Court then formulated a test for what would constitute a religious belief and religious training. That test was stated as follows: "A sincere and meaningful belief which occupies in the life of its possessor a place parallel to that filled by the God of those admittedly qualifying for the exemption,"[14] meaning those belonging to traditions whose view of God is more orthodox. The Justices opined that within this broad concept, the notion of religious training and belief would embrace all religions and exclude "essentially political, sociological, or philosophical views."[15]

Additionally, the Justices recognized the "richness and variety of spiritual life"[16] in the United States. The Court acknowledged Buddhists, Hindus, the Mennonites, and the Amish as part of this wealth of spiritual pluralism. The *Seeger* court also noted that there were many non-mainstream religions that enjoyed First Amendment protection: the Mennonites, the Society of Friends (Quakers), the Amish, the Hutterites, the Buddhists, and the Hindus.[17]

The notion of "God" has been somewhat problematic for the courts. For example, by 1961, the Supreme Court had found that religion was no longer defined by a traditional concept of God, as evidenced by *Torasco v. Watkins* (367 U.S. 488 [1961]). This case was brought by a Maryland appointee to the office of notary public. The appointee was refused his notary commission by the state of Maryland because he refused to declare his belief in God. The U.S. Supreme Court decided this matter in favor of the Plaintiff and stated:

> We repeat and again reaffirm that neither a State nor the Federal Government can constitutionally force a person 'to profess a belief or disbelief in any religion,' Neither can constitutionally pass laws or impose requirements which aid all religions as against nonbelievers...and neither can aid those religions based on a belief in the existence of God as against those religions founded on different beliefs.
>
> (*Torasco*, 495)

The Court additionally noted that there were religions that did not profess a belief in God, such as Buddhism, Taoism, Ethical Culture, and Secular Humanism.[18] This case and in particular, its footnote 11, continue to be controversial. For example, in a Ninth Circuit Court of Appeals case involving the erection of a city park statue of the ancient Aztec Plumed Serpent Quetzacoatl, the court stated that in *Torasco,* the

U.S. Supreme Court had "assumed without deciding that certain non-theistic beliefs could be deemed 'religious,' for First Amendment purposes."[19]

The Supreme Court revisited the concept of a Supreme Being in *Welsh v. United States* (398 U.S. 333 [1970]), another conscientious objector case involving the Military Training Act. Writing for the majority of the Court, Justice Black stated that "the central consideration in determining whether the registrant's beliefs are religious is whether these beliefs play the role of a religion and function as a religion in the registrant's life."[20] Addressing more traditional, or parochial, concepts of religion, Justice Black firmly stated that these do not define what is or is not a religious belief; rather, it is whether one's "moral, ethical, or religious beliefs about what is right and wrong...are held with the strength of traditional religious convictions."[21] Thus, belief in a Supreme Being was no longer necessary under the Act in order to qualify a belief as religious. One of the problems with the conscientious objector cases and their broad findings has been subsequent court interpretations which declare that the findings are applicable only within the context of the Universal Military Training and Service Act: for example, the case *Missouri Church of Scientology v. State Commission of Missouri* (560 S.W.2d 837 [Mo. 1977]). The *Seeger* court itself stated that its decision in that case was being rendered solely in relation to the language of the statute and not otherwise.[22]

Still, some state courts cling tenaciously to the notion that in order to be a religion, a Supreme Being must be present and believed in. As late as 1977, the Missouri Supreme Court in the *Missouri Church of Scientology* case was still asserting that, at a minimum, a religion required belief in a Supreme Being. The Missouri State Supreme Court distinguished *Seeger* and the selective service cases by saying that these were cases involving a specific federal statute and had no applicability to the facts presented in the Church of Scientology matter before them.[23]

For Pagans, the *Missouri Church of Scientology* case is important: It was relied and elaborated upon in depth by the State Tax Commission of

Missouri in its landmark decision of *Ozark Avalon v. Lachner* (Missouri State Tax Commission, Appeal Number 00-525000), which was rendered in 2001. The *Ozark Avalon* tax case involved a Wiccan church in Missouri. A copy of this decision can be downloaded from the Website for the Missouri Department of Revenue at *www.dor.state.mo.us/stc/ozark_avalon_v_lachner.htm*.

Wiccans and other Pagans who profess belief in some sort of deity should take heart. Deep in the Bible belt of the conservative Midwest, the Wiccan church of Ozark Avalon won its battle for a state tax exemption as set forth in the Missouri state constitution and state statutes against the Tax Assessor of Cooper County, Missouri. The evidence before the Missouri State Tax Commission, as compiled by Ozark Avalon, included a list of nineteen exhibits. Those exhibits included an IRS exemption letter, a state certificate of incorporation, the articles of incorporation, written direct testimony of officers of the corporation, and live testimony elicited from one of those officers, Mr. Robert Thomas Dixon, III. The sole issue was whether Ozark Avalon would qualify for the state tax exemption that was reserved for property used for religious, education, or charitable purposes.

Relying on the *Missouri Church of Scientology* case, the state Tax Commission held that under the Missouri constitution and the Missouri taxation statute, the term "religious worship" meant that, at a minimum, there must be a belief in the Supreme Being. In identifying that Supreme Being, however, the Tax Commission stated:

> The term Supreme Being must be given its widest possible reading and definition. It will not suffice for a narrow, strict, technical meaning to be given to this phrase, for a stringent meaning can only result in the government giving benefit to those of one religious faith and denying the same to those of other religious faiths in violation of the Non-establishment Clause of the First Amendment. Such a course of action would have the

effect of a denial of equal protection by preferring some religions over others—an invidious discrimination that would transgress the Due Process Clause of the Fifth Amendment.

(*Ozark Avalon,* State Tax Commission of Missouri, August 8, 2001, 13)

Addressing the issue of whether this Supreme Being can be limited to the god of the Jews, Christians, and Muslims, the Tax Commission stated unequivocally:

> While it might be comforting to Jews, Roman Catholics, Orthodox Catholics, Protestants, and other Christian groups not considered to be Protestants and Muslims that the Supreme Being is the God of Abraham, Isaac, and Jacob–Allah, such a line of demarcation results in those of Buddhist, Hindu, Native American, Taoist, Confucianist and various other religious entities whose Supreme Being is not the God recognized generally by those labeled as Jews, Christians, and Muslims, being denied tax exempt status for their religious sites because theirs is not a religious devotion to the Supreme Being. Such a standard in effect restricts the definition of religious worship or religion to conventional orthodox religions....If on the other hand, the Supreme Being is a Hindu god, then churches, mosques and synagogues throughout the state have been wrongly granted religious exemptions, because of a religious devotion to the wrong Supreme Being.

(*Ozark Avalon,* State Tax Commission of Missouri, August 8, 2001, 12)

The State Tax Commission of Missouri held, in no uncertain terms:

> ...Ozark Avalon's belief encompasses faith in and devo-
> tion to what it considers to be Supreme Being. The form
> of manifestation for Supreme Being in the faith and prac-
> tice of Ozark Avalon is irrelevant. Part and parcel of the
> worship of Ozark Avalon is its recognition of Supreme
> Being–God and Goddess–as contained within the tenents
> of its creed or statement of faith...Ozark Avalon satisfies
> the requirement of devotion to Supreme Being....
>
> (*Ozark Avalon,* State Tax Commission of Missouri,
> August 8, 2001, 13)

How will the Supreme Court react to the notion of a Pagan or Wiccan Goddess? Justice Douglas, in his concurring opinion to the *Seeger* case, has already given us a preview:

> The words "a Supreme Being" have no narrow technical
> meaning in the field of religion. Long before the birth of
> our Judeo-Christian civilization the idea of God had taken
> hold in many forms. Mention of only two—Hinduism
> and Buddhism—illustrates the fluidity and evanescent
> scope of the concept. In the Hindu religion the Supreme
> Being is conceived in the forms of several cult Deities.
> The chief of these, which stand for the Hindu triad, are
> Brahma, Vishnu and Siva. Another Deity, and the one
> most widely worshipped, is Sakti, the Mother Goddess,
> conceived as power, both destructive and creative.
>
> (*Seeger,* 189)

Obviously, judicial bodies have not surrendered to pop culture when defining religions. Relying heavily on the *Seeger* and *Welsh* cases, other federal courts have, in the absence of a requirement of "God," looked to a person's "ultimate concern"—whatever that concern might be—and have used that ultimate concern to shape the notion of religion such that there is no "God" requirement. Such an ultimate concern is more than intellectual and will disregard basic self-interest.[24] An individual possessed of such an ultimate concern will be responding to some sort of inner mentor, whether that be God or a sense of conscience.[25]

Judges continue to filter volumes of facts through this cheesecloth of definitions in order to determine whether certain belief systems and practices are religions, or religious, such that they will merit First Amendment protection. For example, in the case *International Society for Krishna Consciousness v. Barber, et al.* (650 F. 2d 430 [2d Cir. 1981]), the Second Circuit Court of Appeals looked at numerous factors to decide if the Krishnas were practicing a religion meritorious of First Amendment protection. The court found that the Krishna faith had an elaborate and articulate body of religious doctrine; the sect's members forsook the pleasures of the material world, donned strange clothing, altered their diet, rose at 4 a.m. to chant prayers, and endured both scorn and derision from family and friends in the pursuit of their beliefs; the movement had its roots in the diverse and ancient Hindu faith; and thousands of devotees had been attracted from all over the world. The federal appellate court also noted the nonprofit tax status accorded the organization by both the state of New York and the Internal Revenue Service. The court also evaluated the sincerity of the sect's adherents in a rather lengthy analysis and finally concluded that the act of educating unbelievers and then asking for money was, indeed, a religious activity which deserved the protection of the Free Exercise clause.[26]

Interestingly, the *Krishna* court noted that lay courts familiar with Western religions and their traditions of "sacramental rituals and structured theologies are ill equipped to evaluate the relative significance of particular rites of an alien faith."[27] However, Catholic nuns and priests have been wearing strange clothes, getting up at odd hours to perform acts of devotional worship, changing their diet, and enduring the scorn and derision of their families and friends for centuries. Yet, courts do not seem to view Catholicism as "alien."

PAGAN TRADITIONS HAVE SURVIVED THE DEFINITION PROCESS AND BEEN PRONOUNCED "RELIGIONS"

In several important court cases involving Pagan litigants, the Pagan traditions involved have survived the various court tests of "what is a religion" for the purposes of the First Amendment. Unfortunately, none of these cases is a U.S. Supreme Court case. The Supreme Court Justices have not decided this ultimate question as it relates to some of the more prominent Pagan spiritual traditions, such as Wicca/Witchcraft, Druidry, or Asatrú.

Significantly, the courts are not the only governmental entity to favorably treat Pagan traditions. The IRS recognizes a certain number of Pagan organizations as 501(c)(3) not-for-profit organizations that are, in effect, churches. The exact number of these organizations cannot, at this time, be determined. However, this book addresses several of them, including the Church of All Worlds, Camp Gaea, Spirit Weaver's Church, Ozark Avalon, the Sacred Well Congregation, and the Church of the Iron Oak. A search via the Internet reveals many others. Interestingly, there are branches of the Church of Satan which are state-chartered nonprofit corporations. For example, the Legion of Loki is a grotto of the Church of Satan, and the Legion's Website states that they are a Missouri not-for-profit charitable organization. Their home on the Internet can be found at *www.home.ix.netclm.coml-ambrosi/*.

Additionally, the Ordo Templi Orientis (Order of Oriental Templars, or the OTO, as it is more commonly known) has federal tax-exempt status. This organization claims to be the modern heir of Aleister Crowley's Thelemic order. Their Website states that they are a tax exempt religious organization under IRS section 501(c)(3). Their Website can be found at *www.otohq.org/oto/otohq.html.*

THE *HILEAH* CASE

In 1993, the Supreme Court decided a case involving Santeria, which could be characterized as an alternative spiritual tradition; therefore, the case is discussed here. At the center of controversy in *Church of Lukumi*

Babalu Aye, Inc. and Ernesto Pichardo v. City of Hileah (508 U.S. 520 [1993]) was a religious group practicing Santeria, an amalgamation of traditional African nature religions practiced by the Yoruban people and some elements of Roman Catholicism. The Santerians were asserting their right to practice animal sacrifice, an act allegedly in violation of the city's ordinances. In a sweeping decision, the United States Supreme Court found that the ordinances had been specifically enacted to foreclose Santerian worship and animal sacrifice.[28] The ordinances were found to be unconstitutional; the Court held that Santeria was a religion meritorious of First Amendment protection. The Santerians successfully asserted that animal sacrifice was a constitutionally protected religious rite.

Importantly, the Defendant City failed to argue that Santeria was *not* a religion within the meaning of the First Amendment. The Justices noted: "Nor could it."[29] Furthermore, neither the City nor the lower courts (in this case, the federal district court and the federal appellate court), had questioned the sincerity of belief to perform animal sacrifice for religious reasons. No doubt this would have been hard to refute, given that the group had received legal status as a church under Florida law and had purchased land for construction of a temple, a cultural center, and a school, the stated purpose of which was to bring Santeria and its practice of animal sacrifice into the open.

Regarding the notion that animal sacrifice was far fetched, the Justices stated: "Given the historical association between animal sacrifice and religious worship, the integral feature of animal sacrifice to Santerians simply is not bizarre or incredible."[30] To illustrate, the Old Testament reveals that the Jewish tribes practiced animal sacrifice. For example,, in Genesis 22:9-14, Abraham sacrificed a ram that appeared in a thicket rather than sacrifice his son. The Court particularly focused on the Jewish tradition of kosher slaughter of livestock, which was permissible under the city's ordinances. Noting that the First Amendment forbids any "official purpose to disapprove of a particular religion or of religion in general,"[31] the Court went on to analyze the situation at hand.

Before leaving *Hileah*, one aspect of the case bears comment. As distasteful as most modern Pagans find the notion of animal sacrifice, the Santerian rite addressed in this Supreme Court case is obviously not the garden variety "I worship the Devil and drink the blood of animals" kind of pop culture practice upon which most people focus. In this case, the Court afforded the rite the same sort of reverence as the Jewish kosher slaughter and the animal sacrifice practiced in the Old Testament.

THE *DETTMER* CASES

For Pagans, the most important cases involving First Amendment verification of a Pagan tradition are the two *Dettmer* cases: *Dettmer v. Landon* (617 F. Supp. 592 [E.D. Va. 1985]) and *Dettmer v. Landon* (799 F.2d 929 [4th Cir. 1986]). Decided favorably for the Plaintiff at the federal trial level, there were favorable findings in the federal appellate court, as well. In the cases, the terms "Wicca" and "Witchcraft" are used interchangeably. Plaintiff was incarcerated at a Virginia prison. A Wiccan, he claimed that prison officials refused him worship materials: candles, a statue, a white robe, incense, and either sulfur, sea salt or uniodized salt. Plaintiff asserted that this refusal intruded upon his First Amendment right to the free exercise

42 U.S.C. Sec. 1983 is the vehicle through which many civil rights actions are brought. It provides, in pertinent part, as follows: "Every person who, under color of any statute, ordinance regulation, custom, or usage, of any State or Territory of the District of Columbia, subjects, or causes to be subjected, any citizen of the United States or other person within the jurisdiction thereof to the deprivation of any rights, privileges, or immunities secured by the Constitution and laws, shall be liable to the party injured in an action at law, suit in equity, or other proper proceeding for redress...."

of his religion. Plaintiff sued the Deputy Director for the Virginia Department of Corrections under 42 U.S.C. Sec. 1983 following exhaustion of his administrative remedies.

The case was first tried to District Judge Williams of the United States District Court for the Eastern District of Virginia. Based on the evidence presented to him, Judge Williams issued Findings of Fact and Conclusions of Law. These were favorable to Plaintiff. On appeal to the Fourth Circuit by the Defendant Deputy Director of Corrections, the federal appellate court upheld that part of the district court's decision which found that Plaintiff's religious convictions were a doctrine which "must be considered a religion."[32] Those religious convictions arose from the Church of Wicca.

The factual findings made by Judge Williams at the trial level involved a rigorous treatment of Wicca. These findings were based upon evidence presented at trial by the litigants. Specifically, Judge Williams determined that Wiccan Craft or the Church of Wicca was "an ancient faith"[33] and had a "fairly substantial following in Northern Europe around the 10th and 11th centuries."[34] It waned in popularity and became less visible as Christianity waxed. The witch hunts also accounted to its decline, but it did survive in isolated locations until finding a modest popularity in recent times. Judge Williams noted an estimated 10,000–50,000 followers of the Church of Wicca in the United States.

Based on the evidence, Judge Williams found that Wiccans meet to worship in autonomous groups called covens and that principles of belief varied widely from group to group; however, they are "generally guided by a belief structure which appears to relate to 'ultimate' concerns in a manner similar to the belief structures of more conventional religions."[35] Judge Williams focused on other group features: the ceremonial use of meditation, prayer, incense, robes, and candles, the worship of gods, an emphasis on the spiritual development of individual members, and extensive literature and folklore. The Judge stated that these features were "not unlike features of other religious groups."[36]

Judge Williams noted that Plaintiff had been studying Wicca for over six years; he had contacted a Wiccan organization for information; he had purchased educational materials; and he gave uncontradicted testimony that he had been a sincere member of the Wiccan faith for about two years.[37] This last point is important because it means that no evidence or testimony was presented to dispute Plaintiff's assertions that he had been a sincere member of the Wiccan faith for this length of time.

Straining these facts through the filters of the *Seeger* case, the *Yoder* case, and the *Thomas v. Review Board* case, Judge Williams concluded, as a matter of law:

> ...the Church of Wicca is clearly a religion for first amendment purposes. Members of the Church sincerely adhere to a fairly complex set of doctrines relating to the spiritual aspect of their lives, and in doing so they have 'ultimate concerns' in much the same way as followers of more accepted religions. Their ceremonies and leader structure, their rather elaborate set of articulated doctrine, their belief in the concept of another world, and their broad concern for improving the quality of life for others gives them at least some facial similarity to other more widely recognized religions. While there are certainly aspects of Wiccan philosophy that may strike most people as strange or incomprehensible, the mere fact that a belief may be unusual does not strip it of constitutional protection. Accordingly, the Court concludes that the Church of Wicca, of which the plaintiff is a sincere follower, is a religion for the purpose of the free exercise clause.
>
> (*Dettmer*, 617 F. Supp. 592, 596)

The appellate court decision was rendered by Senior Circuit Judge Butzner. First, Judge Butzner affirmed the test used by the District Court in determining whether Wicca was a religion: Did the Church of Wicca occupy a place in the lives of its members which was parallel to that filled by the orthodox belief in God held by religions that were more widely accepted in the United States? The Church of Wicca doctrines addressed ultimate questions of human life such as belief in another world and improving the quality of life for others. The content of Wiccan doctrine paralleled that of more conventional religions, as well. Judge Butzner also commented that Dettmer testified to his belief in a Supreme Being.[38]

The appellate court found that members of the Church of Wicca worshipped individually and corporately. They followed spiritual leaders. Plaintiff sought guidance from these spiritual leaders and testified that he hoped to conduct ceremonies privately and with other inmates. Judge Butzner found that witchcraft had a long history: It was an "ancient pagan faith."[39] He also pointed out that as part of Plaintiff's evidence, Plaintiff introduced a "handbook for chaplains published by the United States, which states that witchcraft enjoyed a following in Northern Europe during the Middle ages as an ancient pagan faith…"[40] Here, the court is obviously referring to the Military Handbook for Chaplains, and obviously, the appellate court relied on this handbook in rendering its decision.

This controversial document is now considered obsolete. Once available on the Internet, the Chiefs of Chaplains of the Service have been directed to remove it and all references to it from their inventories. The document in question was the Department of the Army (DA) Pamphlet 165-13-1, *Religious Requirements and Practices of Certain Selected Groups: A Handbook for Chaplains* (April, 1978).[41]

Judge Butzner swiftly disposed of the Defendant government's position that the Church of Wicca was not a religion. The Defendant argued that the Church of Wicca was "a 'conglomeration' of 'various aspects of the occult, such as faith healing, self-hypnosis, tarot card reading, and spell casting, none of which would be considered religious practices standing alone.'"[42] In response, Judge Butzner stated: "The government argues essentially that because it finds witchcraft to be illogical and internally inconsistent, witchcraft cannot be a religion. The Supreme Court has held to the contrary that 'religious beliefs need not be acceptable, logical, consistent, or comprehensible to others in order to merit First Amendment protection.'"[43]

Additionally, the government asserted that the practice of the beliefs was not religious. The defense characterized Plaintiff's rites "as more akin to meditation than to religion...Wiccan meditation is 'primarily designed to assist the practitioner to master the concept of positive thinking and to find internal contentment.'"[44] Judge Butzner countered by pointing to Plaintiff's testimony that while in meditation, Plaintiff would "'call down power'"[45] from "'the supreme being' and other deities.'"[46] The Judge went on to say: "We agree with the district court...that the Church of Wicca occupies a place in the lives of its members parallel to that of more conventional religions. Consequently, its doctrine must be considered a religion."[47]

Having decided the threshold issue of whether Wicca was a religion, the appellate court proceeded to the second level of analysis: whether to give Plaintiff the ceremonial items he had requested. This was the "free exercise" analysis. On this point, the District Court and the Appellate Court disagreed. In the District Court, Judge Williams found that prisoners worshipping in more conventional religions such as Catholicism and Hinduism were given access to candles, incense, and crosses, and all prisoners were routinely given access to bathrobes and boxing robes. In the federal appellate court, Judge Butzner made a different finding: "[n]o prisoner at the Correctional Center is allowed to possess the items Dettmer wants."[48] Judge Butzner also favorably mentioned the trial testimony of the security chief who outlined the disruption and dangerous uses to which the requested items could be put: sulfur was an explosive ingredient; the white hooded robe resembled Klu Klux Klan robes and might provoke adverse prisoner reaction; candles could be used to make timing devices and impressions of keys; hollow statues could conceal contraband; incense could disguise the odor of marijuana; and a kitchen timer could be used to make a detonation device.[49] On some of these items, Dettmer and the prison officials were able to reach a compromise, but not on the possession of candles, incense, and salt. Regarding these items, Judge Butzner afforded the prison administration a certain amount of latitude to maintain order and discipline in the prison. The government was not required to take the least restrictive means necessary when limiting prisoners' religious rights.[50]

Decided in 1985 and 1986, the *Dettmer* trial and appellate cases evidence a very different treatment of witchcraft than that afforded to a Michigan woman in the case of *People v. Umerska* (94 Mich. App. 799, 289 N.W.2d 858 [1980]). There, the Michigan appellate court dealt at length with a defendant who represented herself as a Witch and who was accused of procuring money under false pretenses. At the time, Michigan had a statute that prevented witness interrogation as to the witness' religion. Ostensibly, this was to prevent juror prejudice. However, the case was tried to a judge and despite the statute, the judge heard testimony regarding witchcraft as a religion from the defendant. This included Defendant's testimony that hers was a religion of perfect love, trust, and harmony without any belief in evil and hexes.

The state appellate court agreed that the trial judge had properly heard this evidence. The appellate court turned to some very unflattering definitions of witchcraft, such as the 1967 *Encyclopedia Britannica* and the 1957 edition of *Black's Law Dictionary*. In the end, the Michigan appellate court stated: "If anything, witchcraft and religion, as those terms are generally understood, are opposites."[51]

It bears comment that modern Pagans seek more modern definitions of these terms. For an excellent modern treatment on Witches, witches, witchcraft, etc., the bench and bar would do well to look to sources such as *The Encyclopedia of Witches and Witchcraft* (2d ed.), by Rosemary Ellen Guiley. Ms. Guiley details the history of the western concept of witches and witchcraft and how this has evolved into the modern practice of a religion: "Along with contemporary Paganism, contemporary Witchcraft has evolved into a sophisticated religious, magical and mystery tradition. Although it has no orthodoxy or dogma, it does hold core beliefs and practices."[52]

THE *RAVENWOOD* CASE

In at least one state supreme court, Wicca has been pronounced a bona fide religion for purposes of the First Amendment. The seminal case arises out of the Georgia Supreme Court: *Roberts v. Ravenwood Church of Wicca* (249 Ga. 348 [1982]). In that case, a Wiccan church known as the House of Ravenwood, which had been recognized by the IRS, was denied a property tax exemption on a three-bedroom house in Fulton County, Georgia, by the Fulton County Tax Assessor and the Joint City-County Board of Tax Assessors. The Fulton County Tax Assessor and the Board claimed that the organization was not a church. Under state statutes, places of religious worship were exempt from the property *ad valorem* tax.

Ravenwood's founder and resident High Priestess, Lady Sintana, gave uncontradicted and unrebutted deposition testimony that detailed Wiccan cosmology and theology. Obviously impressed with this testimony, the court paraphrased it:

> The Wiccan faith is a matriarchal religion which originated in Europe. In this faith, there is a belief in a deity, but not in the sense of an anthropomorphic God. Rather, the Wiccan belief is that there is a primordial, supernatural force which is the creator of the world and universe and which permeates everything therein. In the Wiccan faith, there is a deification of this force, and all individuals are seen as divine sparks from this divinity with a concomitant moral and ethical responsibility to themselves and to everything in the universe....
>
> (*Ravenwood,* 349–350)

Lady Sintana's unrefuted testimony also addressed Sabbat celebrations, together with some basic Wiccan tenets which, according to her, included self-responsibility, karma, a belief in the teachings of Christ, and a lack of belief in the Christian Devil. Paraphrasing Lady Sintana, the court noted: "Adherents to the Wiccan faith do not practice the stereotypical 'double, double toil and trouble' witchcraft, and Voodoo-like curses and hexes play no part in the Wiccan philosophy."[53]

Her testimony also touched upon her training as an ordained minister of the Wiccan faith, together with her ability to perform legal marriages in the state of Georgia. She testified that Ravenwood had status with the IRS as a church. All this testimony was also uncontradicted. Additional evidence before the court revealed that students lived in the house, paid rent, and that the rent was applied to the mortgage. The building was used for ceremonies and worship.

The Georgia Supreme Court acknowledged that evaluating beliefs in order to determine if they are religious beliefs is tricky business but that this must be done in order to determine whether those beliefs exhibit the minimum requirements of a religion. The Georgia Justices then proceeded to quote *Seeger* from page 165 of that decision:

> The definition has been applied liberally, particularly in our modern age when new and unorthodox religious societies and organizations have appeared. Unorthodoxy will not serve to disqualify a religious group from tax exemption, as long as the group holds a sincere and meaningful belief in God occupying in the life of its possessors a place parallel to that occupied by God in traditional religions, and dedicates itself to the practice of that belief [citations omitted].
>
> (*Ravenwood,* 351–352)

Looking at all the evidence, this southern supreme court found: "…we must hold that the activities conducted by Ravenwood do constitute religious worship."[54] On the second tier of examination—whether Ravenwood should have the tax exemption—the court determined that only the portion of the house used primarily for religious purposes qualified for the tax exemption.

Like *Dettmer,* the court in *Ravenwood* used the terms "Wicca" and "Witchcraft" interchangeably. Thus, no distinction was drawn between Wiccans and Witches in these cases. This could be important to future litigation because there is a growing distinction made in Pagan circles as to Wiccans, Witches, and witches. Some Pagans distinguish among these three and arguably, there are some witches who are not even Pagan, but maintain their Christian belief system while practicing a form of folkloric craft involving healing remedies. Anyone wishing to establish their beliefs and practices as a religion meritorious of First Amendment protection must seriously consider the evidence that they present in court and may wish to review the evidence given by Mr. Dettmer and Lady Sintana in their respective cases.

ADDITIONAL WICCA CASES

Other cases view Wicca favorably. In the *Rust* case (discussed later in this chapter), the federal district court of Nebraska counted Wicca among the 22 religions recognized by the Nebraska State Penitentiary. In *Maberry v. McKune* (24 F. Supp.2d 1222 [D. Kansas 1998]), the federal district court of Kansas stated: "Wicca is a religion that is dedicated to the earth and the Goddess."[55] Additionally, this case makes favorable mention of Wicca, Asatrú, Islam, Mormonism, and Native American spiritual beliefs. The court includes them in the same breath as "the Christian umbrella."[56] The court also mentions Thelema and the Ordo Templi Orientis. The Seventh Circuit Court of Appeals has assumed, without deciding, that Wicca is a religion for purposes of the federal employment discrimination statute, which is Title VII.[57] The EEOC has also found Wicca to be a religion for the purposes Title VII.[58] The Ninth Circuit Court of Appeals briefly addressed Wicca/witchcraft in the case of *Brown v. Woodland Joint Unified School District* (27 F.3rd 1373 [9th Cir. 1994]).

There are federal cases that favorably mention Wicca as a religion without deciding the issue. In *Fleischfresser v. Directors of Sch. Dst. 200* (15 F.3rd 680 [7th Cir. 1994]), the Seventh Circuit Court of Appeals analyzed the claims of elementary school parents that centered around the Impressions Reading Series. This series included such authors as C.S. Lewis (*The Chronicles of Narnia*), J.R.R. Tolkien (*The Lord of the Rings*), A.A. Milne (*Winnie the Pooh*), Frank Baum (*The Wizard of Oz*), Maurice Sendak (*Where the Wild Things Are*), and Ray Bradbury (*The Martian Chronicles*).[59]

The concerned parents asserted that the reading series:

> ...fostered "a religions belief in the existence of superior
> beings exercising power over human beings by imposing
> rules of conduct, with the promise and threat of future
> rewards and punishment," and focuses on supernatural
> beings including "wizards, sorcerers, giants and unspeci-
> fied creatures with supernatural powers." The parents also
> claim that use of the series "indoctrinates children in val-
> ues directly opposed to their Christian beliefs by teach-
> ing tricks, despair, deceit, parental disrespect and by
> denigrating Christian symbols and holidays."
>
> (*Fleischfresser,* 683)

In their brief, the parents also alleged that the school was requiring the students to "practice being witches."[60] From a purely common sense point of view, one could turn these arguments on their ear, somewhat, and put the proverbial shoe on the other foot: Every time a public school uses a Christian or Jewish story or scriptural passage, then the school is attempting to force the children into being Christians or Jews. Children who are forced to pray are being forced to practice being Christians. Of course, one wonders if these concerned parents ever read the Bible, which is full of "superior beings" who "exercise power over human beings" through the use of "rules of conduct" which "promise future rewards" and which "threaten with punishment." The most notable of these be-ings, of course, is Jehovah himself. Additionally, the Bible is full of sto-ries about wizards and sorcerers. In Exodus 7:8-15, Moses and Aaron came before Pharaoh where Aaron threw his rod down, and it became a serpent. The king of Egypt then summoned his sorcerers and magicians to do the same. The Philistine Goliath is commonly depicted as a giant, towering over David and the rest of the Hebrews. In 1 Samuel 17:5, he is described as having a height of six cubits and a span.

The court, however, restrained itself and did not make these arguments. The court did comment that if the school were trying to force children to be witches, then one should plead that the children were required to participate in a Pagan religion. Additionally, the court said: "But, it is not enough that certain stories in the series strike the parents as reflecting the religions of Neo-Paganism or Witchcraft, or reference Christian holidays."[61]

By now it should be abundantly clear that the Pagan tradition/spiritual denomination known as Wicca passes constitutional muster. It is a bona fide religion that merits First Amendment protection. Wicca is the Pagan tradition that has received the most treatment in the courts. However, another Pagan tradition was also at the center of a court controversy.

THE *RUST* CASE AND THE ASATRÚ

Regarding the Asatrú, the case *Rust v. Clark* (883 F. Supp. 1293, 1297 [D. Neb. 1995]) is illuminating. In that case, a group of Asatrú prisoners in the Nebraska State Penitentiary sued under Section 1983 of the United States Code to enforce their religious rights. They claimed that they were entitled to the use of the following items in prison: an evergreen tree, Thor's Hammer necklaces, individual stone altars, individual wooden drinking bowls, a cauldron, individual drinking horns, an evergreen branch for each ceremony, an ash spear with a rubber head, Viking swords of soft wood, a sauna, a group hobby card to make religious items, and meats for ritual (these were gourmet in nature and included goose). They also wanted allowance to celebrate 23 holidays (with accompanying feast meals), to celebrate Yule over 12–13 days, to form a culture club, and to leap over a sacred fire.

The district court acknowledged that the State of Nebraska recognized Asatrú as a religion, together with 22 other religions, including Wicca.[62] However, the court also found that there was a compelling state interest in the orderly and safe operation of a prison. The court found that to deny the prisoners these requests was in furtherance of that compelling state interest and that the denial was the least restrictive means of furthering that interest.

THE *DOTY* CASE AND SATANISM

When discussing religion and civil rights, most people comment "That is Devil worship" and assume that the discussion ends there. They could not be more incorrect. Even repugnant religious beliefs must be afforded constitutional protection. A raging debate exists as to whether Satanism is a Pagan tradition. Pagan authors Joyce and River Higginbotham identify three types of Satanists: those who "worship Satan as a Deity of the Judeo-Christian-Muslim pantheon"; "those who belong to the Church of Satan, founded by Anton LaVey in 1966"; and "those who belong to the church of the Temple of Set, founded by Michael Aquino in 1975."[63] By including a discussion of Satanism, I do not attempt to argue that any of these three varieties are Pagan traditions; however, at least one court has dealt with the issue of Satanism as a religion. Therefore, the topic merits some evaluation.

In the case of *Doty v. Lewis* (995 F. Supp. 1081 [D. Ariz. 1998]), a prisoner housed in the highest security unit of an Arizona prison sought possession of certain alleged religious items: candles, incense, a Baphomet tapestry, and two books *The Satanic Bible* by Anton LaVey, and *The Necronomicon Book of Magic and Spells*. In the court's evaluation of the situation, two items were crucial: the Plaintiff's prison record and the standard of review upon which the prison's denial of these items was based.[64]

The court found that Plaintiff had exhibited less than exemplary behavior while in prison and detailed that behavior at great length. He had a history of violence and racially motivated attacks. He exhibited tattoos that were Nazi symbols, and he set items on fire. He created weapons and hid weapons. He also boasted of sacrificing cows before he had been imprisoned.

At the time the *Doty* case was decided, the Religious Freedom Restoration Act (RFRA) had been declared unconstitutional; therefore, the court applied the law as it had existed prior to the enactment of the RFRA. This meant that the prison's refusal to allow the items required a legitimate penological need, not a compelling state interest. The Arizona district court turned to two U.S. Supreme Court cases as the filters through which the facts of the case would be strained and evaluated: *Turner v. Safley* (482 U.S. 78 [1987]); and *O'Lone v. Estate of Shabazz* (482 U.S. 342 [1987]).[65]

On its way to reaching a discussion of each item requested by the Plaintiff, the court briefly visited the issue of Satanism as a religion: "There was no question that at the time the Complaint was filed and at the hearing, Plaintiff sincerely believed in the principles of Satanism. In 1992, Plaintiff officially designated his religion with the Department of Corrections as Satanism."[66] The district court also looked very briefly at *The Satanic Bible* but found it unimpressive as a religious text.

The remainder of the opinion was dedicated to analyzing the issue of whether the disputed items were necessary for Plaintiff to practice his religion. Arguably, the evidence regarding the items was so overwhelmingly in favor of the Department of Corrections that the court saw no reason to address the legitimacy of a LaVey-based form of Satanism as a religion under the First Amendment. The court did not directly declare Plaintiff's form of Satanism a religion, but neither did the court declare that it was not a religion. The case certainly leaves room for a well-presented scenario involving Satanism.

PAGANS AND PRISON

Prisoners seem to do well in proving to federal courts that Wicca is a religion meritorious of First Amendment protection. This occurred in the *Dettmer* case and in the case of *Goodman v. Carter* (2001 U.S. Dis. LEXIS 9213 [U.S. District Court for the Northern District of Illinois, Eastern Division]). Mr. Carter converted to Wicca in prison, but he met with opposition from prison officials when he requested incense, Tarot cards, and a vegetarian diet. In a lengthy decision, the Illinois district court found the prisoner's evidence on whether Wicca was a religion convincing and stated, at footnote 2:

> Wicca, according to exhibits submitted by Goodman, is
> a form of neo-paganism, a belief system and way of life
> based upon a modern reconstruction of pre-Christian

Celtic traditions. Wicca recognizes both male and female manifestations of divinity, and its festal times are tied to the cycles of nature. It emphatically dissociates itself from the popular conception of 'witchcraft' as worship of Satan or evil powers. Wicca has been recognized as a religion for First Amendment purposes.

> *Goodman*, page 2, *citing Dettmer*,
> 799 F.2d 929, 932.

Interestingly, in the *Goodman* case, the prison officials denied the use of Tarot cards and asserted that they were destructive and harmful. The defendants offered no evidence in support of these assertions. The court did not accept this bald assertion. The court stated:

> It does not appear that [the defendant] explained how tarot cards would permit a prisoner to 'control or influence another,' or 'control or influence' him to do what. That is not to deny that there are harmful and destructive religious practices, but they must be shown to be such; they cannot be proscribed because they are 'occult' or 'superstitious' or 'cultic.'
>
> *Goodman*, page 38.

In at least one prisoner case, *Smith v. Hundley* (190 F. 3rd 852, 854, fn. 4 [8th Cir. 1999]), the federal court appeared to accept Seax Wicca as a religion upon little, if any, evidence. In this case, the Eighth Circuit used the terms "Wicca" and "witchcraft" interchangeably. Citing from a readily available dictionary, the Eighth Circuit commented: "Wicca, a form of witchcraft, is centered around nature-oriented practices derived from pre-Christian religions. *See* Random House Webster's Unabridged Dictionary 2172 (2d ed. 1997). Smith is a practitioner of the Seax (or Saxon) sect of Wicca."[67]

Prisoners who believe that their free exercise rights are being infringed upon may file a *pro se* action alleging violation of their constitutional rights. This will probably take the form of a 42 U.S.C. Sec. 1983 action. Such an action will be filed in the federal district court of the district in which their prison is located. Actions of this nature are reviewed by the federal district court judges who may then assign the matter to local counsel admitted to practice before the federal bench in that district.

Wiccan prison ministry in the form of Wiccan prison chaplains has occurred. In December of 2001, a Wiccan was hired by the Wisconsin Department of Correction and is currently working as a chaplain at the Waupun Correctional Institution. Of course, there were public outcries. See Kottke, Colleen, "Wiccan Chaplain Targeted by Attacks," *The Reporter*, at *www.wisinfo.com/thereporter/ news/archive/local_7195409.shtml*.

WICCA AND THE MILITARY

The overall topic of Pagans and the military is a rather complex matter requiring a more in-depth treatment by someone actually in the military and is only briefly touched upon here. There is a Website that specifically deals with Pagans and the military: the Military Pagan Network, located at *www.milpagan.org*.

The Office Chief of Chaplains Web page states:

> The United States Army Chaplain Corps has been accommodating the diverse religious needs of military people for years. All faiths are seen as equal under the Constitution of the United States with the mandate of 'separation of church and state.' This idea is further reinforced by the provision of the First Amendment rights

of citizens to engage in the free exercise of religion, as defined by the practitioners of respective faiths, not by the government...The government has no more recognized the Wiccan faith than it has, for example, the Church of the Lutheran Brethren, the Roman Catholic Church, Judaism, or for that matter, atheism. Even now, Congress is working to establish a law entitled "The Freedom of Religion Protection Act." This is not a freedom of 'some', but of all, religions. We live in a diverse and pluralistic nation. We are not asked to accept any or all religions, merely to respect their right to expression and the exercise of their faith...The Army policy, consistent with public law and Department of Defense policy, is to accommodate free exercise of religion for its members. This is a command responsibility and is executed by the Chaplain Corps. The consistent accommodation of free exercise of religion, within the Army, ensures that readiness, mission, and good order and discipline are enhanced.

Brigadier General Gaylord T. Gunhus, Chaplain, U.S. Army,
Deputy Chief of Chaplains, from his June 2, 1999 letter to
Reverend Robert M. Overgaard, Sr., as found on the August,
1999, Chief of Chaplains Information Letter at
http://www.chapnet.army.mil/infoltr/August.99.htm

The courts of military justice have specifically addressed Wicca and have done so favorably. The seminal case is *United States v. Phillips* (42 M.J. 346 [1995]). Defendant was imprisoned in a North Carolina jail following several violations of the Uniform Code of Military Justice. While in the North Carolina jail, he asked for his books on Wicca, but he was refused these items. The head jailer refused to give Defendant the Wiccan Bible, saying that Wicca "'wasn't a recognized religious practice in the State of North Carolina.'"[68]

The Court of Military Review who initially heard the case stated: "'Wicca is a pagan religion, not unlike the ancient Druid faith, believing in the sacredness of Nature. While not involving a belief in, or worship of Satan, prejudice against Wiccans exists because of popular confusion between witchcraft (which is part of the Wiccan faith) and Satanism'."[69] In support of this statement, the Court of Military Review pointed to the Office of the Chief of Chaplains, Dept. of the Army, *Religious Requirements and Practices of Certain Selected Groups: A Handbook for Chaplains.*

At the initial hearing before the Court of Military Review, there were some evidence problems, and the Defendant became angry with his lawyer. He accused his attorney of failing to represent him competently, and the entire matter came before the United States Court of Appeals for the Armed Forces. The Court of Appeals found that there was no evidence to show incompetence of counsel and there was no Wiccan Bible (there was only a Book of Shadows). The Court of Appeals favorably mentioned the *Dettmer* case, but upheld the initial finding of the Court of Military Review, which was to deny the Defendant the items he asked for.[70] The decision of the appellate court here indicates that the entire matter would have turned out differently had enough evidence been presented at the initial hearing.

The case is important for the concurring opinion of Judge Wiss, who stated: "Several aspects of the provocative issue before this Court are clear. First, Wicca is a socially recognized religion. It is acknowledged as such by the Army. *See* Dept. of the Army (DA) Pamphlet 165-13-1, *Religious Requirements and Practices of Certain Selected Groups: A Handbook for Chaplains* (April, 1978). Further, it is acknowledged as such in courts of law."[71] Judge Wiss cited the *Dettmer* case, and he went on to say that it was "unfortunate"[72] that counsel did not illuminate the trial judge regarding the status that Wicca has.

Some may argue that since the Chaplains Handbook has been withdrawn, there is a cloud over the issue of Pagans in the military. For those who have any doubt about the Army's position on Wicca and religion, Major General Bill Denedinger was quoted by ABC as follows: "Federal courts and statutes decreed that they are an organized religion and thus they fall under the protection of the Constitution."[73]

Some folks still do not respect the right of our military personnel to worship according to the dictates of their conscience. At Ford Hood in Texas, there is a circle of Wiccans who are mostly military personnel. They have routinely dealt with desecration of their ritual site. This desecration has occurred on at least three separate occasions: October 28, 2000; in May, 2001 at Bealtaine; and then at the end of May, 2001. During the October, 2000 event, the limestone altar, weighing several hundred pounds, was broken with a sledge hammer, and its pieces were scattered. At least one piece was marked with a blue cross. Ritual items were stolen, and there was ancillary damage.[74]

The Department of Defense takes a position of accommodating the religious beliefs of military personnel, even if others do not: "A basic principal of our nation is free exercise of religion. The Department of Defense places a high value on the rights of members of the Armed Forces to observe the tenets of their respective religions."[75]

Is it a Free Exercise Clause or an Establishment Clause case?

Whew! After having gotten past deciding whether what we Pagans believe is a religion or not, the next tier of analysis in most religious clause cases is determining whether the case is a Free Exercise Clause case or an Establishment Clause case. We have already encountered this second tier of analysis in some of the preceding cases. However, before we look at some of them again, we need a little background on a few things. Essentially, when you claim that some governmental action is an infringement of your Free Exercise rights, you are basically saying that the government's actions are getting in the way of you practicing your religion as your conscience dictates. When you complain that a government action violates the Establishment Clause, you are saying that the government so favors one religion over another as to establish that religion, which is unconstitutional.

Thus, in the *Fleischfresser* case, a group of Christian parents claimed that the school's use of a certain reading series prevented them from complying with their religious obligation to teach specific values to their children. Those parents also claimed that use of the reading series violated their rights under the Establishment clause. The Plaintiff in *Dettmer* claimed that the prison's failure to give him certain ceremonial objects violated the free exercise of his religion, which was the Church of Wicca.

How do courts analyze these cases after they have gotten past the question of whether what you practice is a religion under the First Amendment? There is a standard of review under which the facts of your case are analyzed; that is, there is a cloth through which your circumstances are strained. That cloth is known as the *standard of review*. And yes, the standard of review for Free Exercise Clause cases and Establishment Clause cases is different. We will look at each of them.

"We guarantee the freedom to worship as one chooses. We make room for as wide a variety of beliefs and creeds as the spiritual needs of man deem necessary. We sponsor an attitude on the part of government that shows no partiality to any one group and that lets each flourish according to the zeal of its adherents and the appeal of its dogma."

Zorach v. Clauson (343 U.S. 306, 313 [1952])

The Free Exercise Clause

The Free Exercise Clause can be excerpted from the First Amendment to the U.S. Constitution to read as follows: "Congress shall make no law...prohibiting the free exercise [of religion]." Ms. French collects quite a compendium of Free Exercise cases in footnote 6 of her previously cited article, "From Yoder to Yoda: Models of Traditional, Modern, and Postmodern Religion in U.S. Constitutional Law." This clause deals with the individual's right to choose among types of religious observance and training, free of state compulsion.[76] One scholar states:

> The core of the free exercise clause is voluntarism—the inviolability of conscience. The free exercise clause was at the very least designed to guarantee freedom of conscience by preventing any degree of compulsion in matters of belief. It prohibited not only direct compulsion but also any indirect coercion which might result from subtle discrimination; hence it was offended by any burden based specifically on one's religion.
>
> ("Toward a Constitutional Definition of Religion," 91 HARV. L. REV. 1056 [1978], 1059)

The standard of review under the Free Exercise Clause has undergone quite a bit of change in recent years. From 1963 to 1990, the Supreme Court said that a balancing test was to be used; that is, the burden placed on the citizen's religious liberty was to be balanced against the government's compelling interest in regulating that liberty. This was the test asserted in *Sherbert v. Verner* (374 U.S. 398 [1963]), when the United States Supreme Court stated: "Government may neither compel affirmation of a repugnant belief...nor penalize or discriminate against individuals or groups because they hold religious views abhorrent to the authorities."[77] It was in effect until 1990. This is obviously also the standard of review in the *Int'l Society of Krishna Consciousness* case.

Then, in 1990, the United States Supreme Court changed the standard of review. In the case of *Employment Division v. Smith* (494 U.S. 872 [1990]), involving a Native American's right to smoke peyote as part of his religious practice, the Court switched over to a neutrality test. This did not last long: Congress enacted the Religious Freedom Restoration Act in 1993, thereby requiring the courts to switch back to the standard asserted in *Sherbert*.[78] However, the United States Supreme Court declared the RFRA unconstitutional in the case *City of Boerne v. Flores* (521 U.S. 507, 117 S. Ct. 2157 [1997]).[79]

So, where does this leave the status of constitutional review when handling Free Exercise cases? What standard of review is to be used? One commentator suggests that the standard of review has reverted back to the neutrality test of *Employment Division v. Smith,* cited earlier.[80] Thus, as noted in the *Doty* case, the standard of review in Free Exercise matters reverts to the standard in effect immediately before passage of the RFRA.[81]

And what standard is that? It is the neutrality standard as asserted in the 1990 *Smith* case: The law that you are complaining about must be a neutral law of general applicability. If it is not a neutral law of general applicability, then it impedes your Free Exercise rights and is unconstitutional. In this situation, you usually win. If the court finds the law or asserted governmental action to be a neutral law of general applicability, then it does not impede your Free Exercise rights, and it is constitutional. In this situation, you usually lose.

"Government may neither compel affirmation of a repugnant belief...nor penalize or discriminate against individuals or groups because they hold religious views abhorrent to the authorities." *Sherbert v. Verner* (374 U.S. 398, 402 [1963])

THE ESTABLISHMENT CLAUSE

The Establishment Clause can be excerpted from the First Amendment of the U.S. Constitution as follows: "Congress shall make no law respecting an establishment of religion..." What is this clause all about? In the case of *Lee v. Weisman* (505 U.S. 577 [1992]), the United States Supreme Court stated that the Establishment Clause was inspired by a historical lesson: "that in the hands of government what might begin as a tolerant expression of religious views may end in a policy to indoctrinate and coerce."[82]

What is the standard of review for an Establishment Clause case? Like its sister, the Free Exercise Clause, the Establishment Clause has undergone considerable change over the years. However, in 1971, the Supreme Court put forth a three-pronged test for neutrality in the case of *Lemon v. Kurtzman* (403 U.S. 602, 612–613 [1971]). This is known as the *Lemon* test.

A recent Establishment Clause case involved the Chief Justice of the Alabama State Supreme Court. He erected a monument to the Ten Commandments in the rotunda of the Alabama State Judicial Building in 2001. The federal district court for the Middle District of Alabama, Northern Division (Judge Myron H. Thompson), used the *Lemon* test in this case and found that the erection of the religious monument in the state court building was unconstitutional. The federal district set forth the *Lemon* test: In order for the offensive practice to survive an Establishment Clause challenge under *Lemon*, that practice must have a secular purpose; the principal or primary effect of the practice must neither advance nor inhibit religion; and the offensive practice must not foster an excessive government entanglement with religion. [83]

An example of an Establishment Clause case involving Pagans is that of Wiccan Cynthia Simpson. She asked the Chesterfield County, Virginia Board of Supervisors to add her name to a list of clergy for the performance of invocations at the opening of Board meetings. They turned her down. In their response, the Board indicated that since Wicca was a neo-pagan religion that was polytheistic in its recognition of pre-Christian deities, and since invocations were usually made to a divinity consistent with a Judeo-Christian divinity, the Board would not recognize Ms. Simpson's request. [84] This situation has evolved into a lawsuit, which is currently pending in the United States District Court for the Eastern District of Virginia: *Cynthia Simpson v. Chesterfield County Board of Supervisors*, United States District Court for the Eastern District of Virginia, Richmond Division, Docket Number 3:02CV888. If you are curious about this case, call the clerk of courts for the Eastern District of Virginia in Richmond, and give the clerk the docket number. You may be able to obtain copies of pleading filed in the court.

BEFORE WE GET OUT OF THIS FIRST AMENDMENT BUSINESS, IS THERE ANYTHING ELSE I SHOULD KNOW?

Yes, there is. Some people might believe that in the assertion of their religious freedom, they can wave their ritual blades around in public or perform public ceremony in the nude. They will say, "First Amendment freedom of religion" and believe that it clothes them with immunity from legal prosecution. Not true. First, let's use our common sense here. It should be obvious that no one has an absolute religious right. For example, where would we be if all the people who took Biblical scripture literally acted upon it and then defended their actions based on some cockamamie notion of absolute religious freedom? Obviously, we cannot allow mobs of people to stone adulterers or to round up the Witches and kill them. We can't allow Hindu widows to throw themselves on funeral pyres or Asatrú adherents to set flaming boats carrying corpses adrift on the local pond. In the wake of the tragic events of September 11, 2001, one wonders if we can allow schools to teach doctrines of hate toward certain groups in society. Hate crimes are illegal in many states. Then, there is the issue of sedition, which is a federal offense. So, there is no absolutely right to any of the freedoms we enjoy.

Unsurprisingly, this is also the position taken by the Supreme Court, and they established this position very early:

> But the possession and enjoyment of all rights are subject to such reasonable conditions as may be deemed by the governing authority of the country essential to the safety, health, peace, good order and morals of the community. Even liberty itself, the greatest of all rights, is not unrestricted license to act according to one's will. It is only freedom from restraint under conditions essential to the equal enjoyment of the same right by others. It is then liberty regulated by law.

(*Crowley v. Christensen*, 137 U.S. 86, 89 [1890])

Thus, a large piece of the whole religious freedom pie has already been sliced out. The government—state and federal—can limit personal freedoms, such as religious freedom, for community safety, health, peace, good order, and morals. It is readily apparent that the government can and does place limitations on religion in America.

As we have already seen, the Mormons found this out back in 1878 when a Mormon man with more than one wife was successfully prosecuted for bigamy. This was the *Reynolds* case, where the conflicting issues were personal religious freedom in the form of practicing polygamy and proper governance of the Territories. The Court wasted no time in establishing which was paramount: the duty of the Congress to peaceably govern the Territories took the front seat. The Mormons and their religious practices took the back seat. Polygamy, which was essentially a non-Western concept and practice, would not be incorporated into life in the Territories. The Court made a distinction between religious belief and religious practice, saying that the Mormons could believe in polygamy as part of their religious theology, they just could not practice it. The Court also stated that the U.S. government would not countenance human sacrifice or the practice of self-immolation by wives of dead husbands.

In the later case of *Cantwell v. Connecticut* (310 U.S. 296 [1940]), the Court went on to refine this distinction. Regarding religious acts, the Court stated: "Conduct remains subject to regulation for the protection of society. The freedom to act must have appropriate definition to preserve the enforcement of that protection."[85] For us, the translation is this: No one can tell you what to believe. You may believe what you want; however, you are not always free to act upon it.

In this manner, the Court has established a scale that constantly measures the balance between religious freedom and the obligations of government. This balancing act has taken several very interesting twists and turns in the last 200 years. For example, in cases involving religious sects and the rights of parents to absent their children from public schools under the aegis of religious belief, the cauldron containing the disparate ingredients of religious freedom, parental rights, and the state's interest in some form of universal education is always boiling. These cases continue to present prime examples of how the courts have sought to balance what appear to be absolute rights against compelling state interests.[86] As demonstrated by the *Reynolds* case, religious freedom is not without limits.

Religion and morals are very much live issues today. For example, in 1998, two Texas men were arrested and fined for participating in consensual sex acts in one of their homes. They were convicted under the Texas sodomy law. The United States Supreme Court has agreed to hear this case. However, attorneys arguing against review by the Supreme Court asserted that the states should determine what particular conduct is immoral such that the immoral conduct warrants the imposition of legal sanctions. In 1998, the Alabama State Supreme Court denied custody of a child to a lesbian mother and as part of its supportive reasoning, stated that the mother was engaging in deviate sexual intercourse under the state's anti-sodomy law; further, the mother's lesbian relationship was not moral in the eyes of a majority of citizens.[87]

OKAY, WHAT LIMITATIONS ARE PLACED ON MY RELIGIOUS FREEDOM?

Government limitations on religious freedom are widespread and spring from a variety of legitimate government concerns. Chief among these government concerns are the promotion of health, safety, and general welfare. In fact, the power of the government to legislate in these areas is pretty much beyond doubt. Regarding Pagans, some of these broad concepts have had some pretty specific consequences. For example, the power of the government to enact zoning ordinances governing the various uses for property comes under the umbrella of the government's power to act in its executive capacity. Thus, zoning ordinances can limit church operations. Read Chapter 7 for more about land use.

The power of the government to legislate regarding the prison population is also a shield for use of government power to limit religious practice. Remember the *Rust* case, where a group of Asatrú prisoners in the Nebraska State Penitentiary sued under Section 1983 of the United States Code to enforce their religious rights? They wanted to use a number of items in prison but were denied access to them. The district court acknowledged that the State of Nebraska recognized Asatrú as a religion, together with 22 other religions, including Wicca. Yet, the court also found that there was a compelling state interest in the orderly and safe operation of a prison. The court found that to deny the prisoners these requests was in furtherance of that compelling state interest and that the denial was the least restrictive means of furthering that interest. The parallel Wicca case involves the Plaintiff in the *Dettmer* case.

I would like to stress that Pagans are not the only folk to come up against governmentally imposed limitations on personal religious freedom. Take the restrictions imposed on child rearing and education, for example. The religious beliefs of the Jehovah Witnesses have had to take a back seat to the health and safety of their children. There is a vast wealth of cases involving this particular religious sect and its ongoing battle with the government regarding medical care to be afforded Jehovah Witness children. The Supreme Court addressed the issue of religion, medicine, and children directly in 1944: "The right to practice religion freely does not include liberty to expose the community or the child to communicable disease or the latter to ill health or death."[88] For the Jehovah Witnesses, this has meant that blood transfusions can be given to Jehovah Witness children over the religious objections of the parents.[89]

Hey, I am an ordinary Pagan!
What does all this mean to me?

As our discussion illustrates, there are two aspects to freedom of religion in America that are anchored in the First Amendment: the Establishment Clause and the Free Exercise Clause. First, neither the federal government nor the state governments may establish religion. Second, you may believe whatever you want, but you are not free to act on those beliefs because government is entitled to restrict activity as necessary for the safe and orderly administration of society. You may not be guaranteed as much "free exercise" as you would like to have, but you get as much as everyone else.

You must vigorously and actively defend your rights under the First Amendment because no one else is going to do it for you. People of color have long known this. So have many of the other religious sects who have, over the years, asserted their religious rights: Jews, Muslims, the Amish, Jehovah Witnesses, Catholics, Mennonites, and Mormons. As a Pagan, you are no different from the rest of these folks. Your beliefs may be a little less orthodox than everyone else's, but there is a real reluctance by the courts to pooh-pooh the religious beliefs of its citizenry. If faced with a situation that you believe is truly discriminatory, you must be prepared to stand up and fight for what you believe. You cannot disappear into your cauldron or fly away on your broom and think that everything is going to magically resolve itself in your favor. Education regarding your rights is critical to their exercise. It will eventually be up to you, one day, to educate someone else. Be prepared.

The history of the conflict between government and religion shows us that there is a continuous struggle between what the Supreme Being (who or whatever that is) ordains and what government demands as its due. The age-old conflict of what belongs to God and what belongs to the State is still very much with us. A historical review of American case and statutory law reveals that the struggle between government and religion did not end with the establishment of a constitutional form of government. The interests of government and of religion continue to be at loggerheads with one another. Mercifully, we have better referees for the fight than before the days of the Constitution. When you find yourself in a legal jam involving religion, you cannot quote the First Amendment and believe that all issues are thereby resolved in your favor. We would be thinking like children if we thought that we may do whatever we please, whenever we please, to whomever we please. After all, we don't want everyone else doing that to us.

CHAPTER 4

PAGANS AND CHILD CUSTODY

INTRODUCTION

In my experience as a human being, as a Pagan, and as a lawyer, the most painful situations faced by Pagans are those that involve children. Other than the fear of losing a job, the fear of losing one's children due to religious bias is the single greatest agony with which a Pagan must cope. Pagan parents are afraid that they are going to lose their children in a custody dispute. Pagan parents are afraid that an investigator from the Division of Social Services is going to appear at the doorstep with the police and take their children away. Pagans are genuinely concerned with these issues and rightly so. As much as I would like to say that their fears are without foundation, I simply cannot. People do unspeakable things to one another and to children, all allegedly in the best interests of the child, and whether the parents are actually Pagan may not matter at all.

In dealing with Pagans and child custody, many Pagans claim that the courts are not tolerant of Pagan traditions and practices. Given the fact that most courts assert the general rule that religion should not be a deciding factor in awarding custody,[1] a lot of Pagans scratch their heads and wonder how this can be. These cases are difficult for the courts, as well. On the other hand, there are Pagan folk who claim religious discrimination in the struggle for custody or that their children have been taken from them on the basis of discrimination. In some of these cases, however, a review of all the evidence reveals that there were plenty of truly good reasons to remove a child from a Pagan parent's custody.

"Courts have repeatedly held that custody cannot be awarded solely on the basis of the parents' religious affiliations and that to do so violates the First Amendment to the United States Constitution...On the other hand, a parent's actions are not insulated from the domestic relations court inquiry just because they are based on religious beliefs, especially actions that will harm the child's mental or physical health." *Pater v. Pater* (63 Ohio St.3rd 393, 588 N.E.2d 794, 798 [1992]

So, what is the problem here? As we have previously seen in our discussion of constitutional law, the problem is one of competing interests: the constitutional rights of the parents to raise children as they choose (which includes religious inculcation and upbringing) the compelling interests of the state relative to the "public safety, peace, order, or welfare," the rights of children to exercise their religion, the morals of the community, and finally—but certainly not least—the best interests of the children themselves.[2] In an increasingly eclectic world where religion is concerned, the courts are called upon more often to look at religion in matters involving child custody. However, they have been doing it for quite a while, as the age of some of these cases indicates. Although certainly not the oldest case of its kind, the Missouri case involving Laura Doyle dates back to 1884. The choice of Solomon—to which alleged parent is a child awarded—has been with us for a long time. Jews and Christians, snake handlers and followers of Islam, the Jehovah's Witnesses, and the Seventh Day Adventists—all have been fighting this fight in the American court system and have substantially laid out the legal precedents that Pagans will now encounter.

So, does the court examine religion in child custody cases? Yes, they do, no matter how much "religion does not count" language there is floating around out there. If a court wants to hear all the gruesome details about a parent's religion and how it affects the kids, the court is going to hear it. There is some rather broad language out there indicating that courts are, indeed, very interested in the spiritual welfare of children. For example, in the case of *Cushman v. Lane* (224 Ark. 934, 277 S.W. 2d 72, 74 [1955]), the Arkansas Supreme Court stated that the best interests of the child involve the physical, moral, and spiritual well being of the child. In *Nonnenman v. Elshimy* (615 A.2d 799, 801 [1992]), the Superior Court of Pennsylvania stated that courts recognize a child's spiritual welfare as a factor in determining custody and visitation. In the case of *Waites v. Waites* (567 S.W. 2d 326, 333 [Mo. 1978]), the Missouri Supreme Court stated:

> Inquiry into religious beliefs *per se* is impermissible; inquiry into matters of child development as impinged upon by religious convictions is permissible, as, for example, where a parent might properly be asked whether he or she would refuse to permit the child to attend a school class where evolution is taught; or where religion is being used as a subterfuge, as, for example, an alleged religious tenet which advocates shoplifting as a means of helping the needy.

(*Waites*, 333)

"Great!" you say. "How do I make sense out of this mess?" Well, first things first, and the best place to start is at the beginning. There are Websites that analyze child custody and religion. For example, see *www.nolo.com/lawcenter/ency/article.cfm.* The Nolo.com Website specifically addresses the issue of child custody and religion.

LET'S START WITH THE CONSTITUTION

There is no language in the U.S. Constitution that addresses this issue outright. However, in the case of *Troxel v. Granville* (530 U.S. 57, 120 S. Ct. 2054 [2000]), the Supreme Court found that parents have a fundamental liberty interest in the rearing of their children. This fundamental interest was recognized as early as 1925 in the case of *Pierce v. Society of Sisters* (268 U.S. 510 [1925]). This interest stems from the Fourteenth Amendment of the federal Constitution, which states in pertinent part: "No state shall...deprive any person of life, liberty or property without due process of law."[3] Also remember that the Fourteenth Amendment operates to make the First Amendment applicable to the states, so the First Amendment also comes into play. The courts in the state of Massachusetts have embellished this concept: "The parents together have freedom of religious expression and practice which enters into their liberty to manage the familial relationships."[4]

The *Troxel* case affords an excellent lesson in the constitutional history of the notion that parents have certain fundamental rights where their children are concerned.[5] It should be remembered that children also have a right to practice their religion, as asserted by the U.S. Supreme Court in the case of *Prince v. Massachusetts* (321 U.S. 158, 165 [1944]).

And now, one of the big questions: Are these fundamental liberties absolute? Absolutely not, especially where there are minor children involved. The Supreme Court Justices also addressed this aspect of parental rights in the *Prince* case at pages 166-167: The parents' right to practice their religion freely does not include the liberty to expose children to ill health or death. In the case *Wisconsin v. Yoder* (406 U.S. 205 [1972]), the Justices commented that the authority of parents in the arena of religious upbringing might be encroached upon, only upon a demonstrated or inferred threat of "physical or mental harm to the child, or to the public safety, peace, order, or welfare."[6] Essentially, the Federal Constitution and the state constitutions permit limitation on an individual's liberties in the face of a compelling interest, such as the welfare of a child in a custody case.

Thus, the door is opened to the review by the courts of religion in the child custody arena. However, before leaving this tier of the discussion, we should also remember that it is not only the Federal Constitution that is applicable in these cases. Litigants need to look at the state constitutions in their home states as well. The State has the power to impinge upon the constitutional rights of parents to raise children and to provide religious training where there is a "substantial threat" to the mental and physical health of the child or where there is a substantial threat to the public safety, peace, order, or welfare. As the Supreme Court of Washington has stated: "[w]e do not doubt the right of the state to suppress religious practices dangerous to morals, and presumably those also which are inimical to public safety, health and good order...."[7] At these twin pinnacles, nothing is sacred, and certainly not the religious beliefs of the parents.

"We reiterate our determination that the Missouri Constitution contemplates a strict and pervasive severance between religion and the state. Any suggestion that a state judicial officer were favoring or tending to favor one religious persuasion over another in a child custody dispute would be intolerable to our organic law. Judges should not even give the appearance of such preference or favor." *Waites*, 333 *Waites v. Waites* (567 S.W. 2d 326, 333 [Mo. 1978])

But if the Court Looks at my Religion, they have to be Impartial, Right?

Remembering also that there is a prohibition against establishing religion, the courts profess a position of strict impartiality where religion is concerned; that is, they state over and over again that they will not address the merits of the various religions' faiths. The state of Texas offers several cases[8] on the proposition that the religious practices of a parent should not affect that parent's right to custody, as long as his or her beliefs are legal and moral. Although we may all agree on notions of public safety, peace, order, or welfare, we might not all agree on the notion of morals. The moral well-being of children is also a matter of concern for the courts, usually encompassed within the notion of a child's best interests.[9]

"The law is absolutely impartial in matters of religion." *McLaughlin v. McLaughlin*, 20 Conn. Supp. 274, 132 A.2d 420, 422 (1957)

There are Two Main Considerations after Impartiality

Okay, the courts can review a parent's religious choices where children are concerned, and they have to be impartial. Now what? Two things have to be considered at this point: first, that the states intervene in order to protect and serve the "best interests" of the child; and second, that there must be a demonstrated threat of some sort. In the case *Felton v. Felton* (418 N.E. 2d 606 [1981]), the Massachusetts Supreme Court stated that the best interests of the child are to be promoted, and if the parents disagree, then some limitation of the parental liberty may be involved in order to work in the best interests of the child. In the same case, the Court stated that harm from conflicting religious instruction and/or practice cannot be simply assumed or surmised; rather, it must be demonstrated in detail.[10]

How, then, do the courts balance all these competing interests and liberties? What the parents want? What the kids want? What the state thinks will be in the best interests of the kids? For mere mortals and non-lawyer types, this appears to be a very perplexing coil. Mercifully, judges have help in nearly every state in navigating their way through these competing interests from the individual state legislatures. In many states, the legislative bodies have drafted statutes outlining the factors to be considered when determining custody of children. The overriding theme is "the best interests" of the child. This all sounds easy, right?

WHAT DOES THIS MEAN, "THE BEST INTERESTS" OF THE CHILD?

The short answer is that "the best interests of the child" is the over-reaching consideration for the judge in any individual case. The judge weighs the testimony and evidence before her/him and strains it through the cheesecloth of factors enunciated by each state's statute or constellation of case law. This is all done in an effort to serve "the best interests of the child." Basically, the judge before whom your case is heard at the local level is the initial arbiter of the situation: She/he weighs the various factors in either a statutorily defined equation or an equation that is gleaned from the applicable case law in the state. The state statute lists the factors to be considered by the judge. Based on the evidence presented, the judge sifts through all the factors, and then the judge determines how placement with one parent or the other will serve "the best interests of the child." The judge then issues an Order or decree that sets forth child custody. Again, there is the issue of the evidence presented in a specific case, and you cannot forget that what you practice and believe must first be qualified as a religion in order to merit any of the First Amendment protections.

Do all the state statutes look alike, contain the same features, or sound alike? No. Why is this? Because the state law—statutory and/or case law—determines child custody and the procedures used to determine the best interests of the child differ from state to state. This is not cookie cutter law. The statutes are not cut from the same mold, and state legislatures are always changing them. Also the cases can differ widely. This is why it is imperative that a Pagan involved in a child custody dispute has competent legal counsel with expertise in the subject of child custody in their state. It would probably be preferable to retain an attorney from within the county where the hearing will occur. You want an attorney who has experience with these matters in the court where your case is being heard and before the judge who has been assigned your case.

To demonstrate the wide disparity in how the statutes are drafted, let us look first at the child custody statute in the state of Michigan. It provides that the best interest of the child is a combination of the following factors, which the court must closely consider. The statute then sets forth 12 factors as follows:

> § 25.312(3). "Best interests of child" defined.
> Sec. 3. As used in this act, "best interests of the child" means the sum total of the following factors to be considered, evaluated, and determined by the court:
> (a) The love, affection, and other emotional ties existing between the parties involved and the child.
> (b) The capacity and disposition of the parties involved to give the child love, affection, and guidance and to continue the education and raising of the child in his or her religion or creed, if any.
> (c) The capacity and disposition of the parties involved to provide the child with food, clothing, medical care or other remedial care recognized and permitted under the laws of this state in place of medical care, and other material needs.
> (d) The length of time the child has lived in a stable, satisfactory environment, and the desirability of maintaining continuity.
> (e) The permanence, as a family unit, of the existing or proposed custodial home or homes.

(f) The moral fitness of the parties involved.

(g) The mental and physical health of the parties involved.

(h) The home, school, and community record of the child.

(i) The reasonable preference of the child, if the court considers the child to be of sufficient age to express preference.

(j) The willingness and ability of each of the parties to facilitate and encourage a close and continuing parent-child relationship between the child and the other parent or the child and the parents.

(k) Domestic violence, regardless of whether the violence was directed against or witnessed by the child.

(l) Any other factor considered by the court to be relevant to a particular child custody dispute.

Mich. Stat. Ann. Sec. 25.312(3)

To contrast, the Missouri statute is written quite differently:

2. The court shall determine custody in accordance with the best interests of the child. The court shall consider all relevant factors including:

(1) The wishes of the child's parents as to custody and the proposed parenting plan submitted by both parties;

(2) The needs of the child for a frequent, continuing and meaningful relationship with both parents and the ability and willingness of parents to actively perform their functions as mother and father for the needs of the child;

(3) The interaction and interrelationship of the child with parents, siblings, and any other person who may significantly affect the child's best interests;

(4) Which parent is more likely to allow the child frequent, continuing and meaningful contact with the other parent;

(5) The child's adjustment to the child's home, school, and community;

(6) The mental and physical health of all individuals involved, including any history of abuse of any individuals
involved. If the court finds that a pattern of domestic violence has occurred, and, if the court also finds that awarding custody to the abusive parent is in the best interest of
the child, then the court shall enter written findings of fact
and conclusions of law. Custody and visitation rights shall
be ordered in a manner that best protects the child and the
parent or other family or household member who is the
victim of domestic violence from any further harm;
(7) The intention of either parent to relocate the principal
residence of the child; and
(8) The wishes of a child as to the child's custodian.

MO.V.A.M.S. Sec. 425.375(2)(1)–(8)

Perhaps the most striking difference between the two statutes is the
failure of the Missouri law to mention the word "religion." Does this
stop the Missouri courts from looking at religion as a factor? No, not at
all. As an example, let's really have a look at the *Waites* case.

THE *WAITES* CASE

There, the father was a Baptist and the mother was a converted Jehovah Witness who told the court that she would raise the couple's two
infant daughters in her faith. The trial judge awarded custody to the
father. Upon review in the Missouri Supreme Court, the justices determined that the trial court had given the children to the father due to a
pronounced and demonstrated dislike for Jehovah's Witnesses. This was
simply abhorrent to the Missouri justices, and they placed great emphasis on the state constitution, which provided that " 'no preference shall be
given to nor any discrimination made against any church, sect or creed of
religion, or any form of religious faith or worship.' "[11]

Having determined that the trial judge had committed error, the
justices then had to determine whether to remand the case to the trial

judge or decree custody outright. The justices determined custody outright, and they granted custody to the mother. In support of this decision, the justices relied upon the uncontroverted testimony from the trial. That testimony revealed that the mother was "a loving mother to these young girls...who kept herself regularly employed in an effort to adequately support them. The testimony showed that she regularly spent her time with the children. She read to them, taught, them, kept them with her while she did household chores, took the girls on outings to the zoo and on picnics, kept them clean, fed, and disciplined, as well as provided Bible training consistent with her religious faith."[12]

In contrast, the evidence from the trial revealed the following about the father:

> Respondent has been drifting from job to job, having been employed in at least four different jobs during the last five years. He was asked to leave his job with the Grandview police department after being involved with the sale of beer to minors and was placed on probation at the Blue Springs police department as a result of having threatened appellant's life with his police revolver which threat was made in the presence of the older daughter. Uncontroverted evidence showed that respondent had offered and given alcoholic beverages to the older daughter (now not yet 14 years old). Respondent kept his own religious literature in the family home and like appellant, engaged in door-to-door preaching for his own religious persuasion.
>
> (*Waites,* 334)

I suppose the moral to this particular Missouri story is that you should not give liquor to minors, not even your own kids, threaten people with revolvers, and then attempt to get your kids in a custody case.

Now, let's look at the Massachusetts statute:

> In making an order or judgment relative to the custody
> of children, the rights of the parents shall, in the absence
> of misconduct, be held to be equal, and the happiness
> and welfare of the children shall determine their custody.
> When considering the happiness and welfare of the child,
> the court shall consider whether or not the child's present
> or past living conditions adversely affect his physical,
> mental, moral or emotional health.

M.G.L.A. Ch. 208, Section 31

The seminal case involving the statute is the case of *Kendall v. Kendall* (426 Mass. 238, 687 N.E.2d 1228 [1997]). There, the Plaintiff wife was Jewish when she married her Defendant husband, who was Catholic at the time. Before they married, husband and wife decided that their children would be raised Jewish. During the course of the marriage, the husband converted to a fundamentalist Christian denomination and the wife adopted Orthodox Judaism. The spouses' religious differences eventually polarized them, and the wife filed for a divorce. By this time, the eldest child had begun studying Orthodox Judaism and adhering to its principles. The younger child had a strong sense of Jewish identity. The father wanted his children to "accept Jesus Christ."[13] The divorce decree did not permit the father to impose his religious beliefs on his children should these beliefs cause significant emotional distress or worry in the children about themselves or their mother. The father was persistent, however, and the mother filed a complaint against the father in probate court for contempt of the divorce judgment.

The probate court judge appointed a psychologist as a Guardian ad Litem (GAL)/investigator, evaluator. The contents of his report were given significant weight by the Supreme Court and are telling, indeed. The father took the children to his church where they were taught that if they did not accept the teachings of the Boston Church of Christ, that they were damned to go to hell with gnashing of teeth and weeping. This caused the eldest child substantial worry and upset. The father objected to his children being taught the history of the Holocaust and insisted that all people who did not accept his beliefs about life and existence were sinners destined for tortuous punishment. The father cut off his eldest son's side burns (payes) and threatened to cut the tzitzitz (fringes) from his clothing. The eldest child was made to do things on the Shabbas' that he was not supposed to do. Consequently, the eldest child experienced a decline in motivation and academic performance, in addition to significant emotional distress. The GAL also found that the younger child was experiencing emotional distress related to the parental conflict.

In essence, the husband had put the children in a position of having to choose either being Jewish or members of the Boston Church of Christ, and to impose such a choice upon the children would probably have the effect of truly upsetting the child, as well as presenting him with a damaging representation of the Jewish faith. The Supreme Court agreed with the trial judge and affirmed the divorce decree of the probate judge, which was rather stringent:

> Each parent shall be entitled to share his/her religious beliefs with the children with restrictions as follows: neither may indoctrinate the children in a manner which substantially promotes their...alienation from either parent or their rejection of either parent. The [defendant] shall not take the children to his church (whether to church services or Sunday School or church educational programs); nor engage them in prayer or bible study if it promotes rejection rather than acceptance, of their mother or their own Jewish self-identity. The [defendant] shall not share his religious beliefs with the children if those beliefs cause the children significant emotional distress or worry about their mother or about themselves. Thus, for example, [the defendant] may have pictures of Jesus

Christ hanging on the walls of his residence, and that will not serve as any basis for restricting his visitation with his children. But, [the defendant] may not take the children to religious services where they receive the message that adults or children who do not accept Jesus Christ as their lord and savior are destined to burn in hell. By way of further example, [the defendant] may not shave off [Ariel's] payes.

(*Kendall,* 1231, citing the judgment of divorce
rendered by the probate judge)

I suppose that most Pagan parents are thinking to themselves: Would our Pagan religion have been accorded the same respect as Judaism in this case such that our children who identify themselves as Pagan would not be forced to endure hell fire and damnation lectures from Christian fundamentalist relatives?

WHAT ABOUT THE SHOWING
OF A SUBSTANTIAL THREAT?

In general, the courts are clear: It is unconstitutional and thus, legally impermissible to award custody based solely on the issue of religion. However, when religion *is* analyzed as a factor, how is it analyzed? This is the real nitty-gritty of religion in a child custody dispute. Many states will assess the merits of a religion as they relate to the child only upon a showing of some negative impact upon the child or, as the United States Supreme Court has stated, upon a showing of a substantial threat.[14] The complaining party who wants to take the kids away from the Pagan parent has to prove that there is a substantial threat to the kids or that there is some clear evidence of substantial harm. In some states, the standard for review is not that strict. It would be wonderful if all the states were uniform in the application of such principles as "showing of a substantial threat" or "clear evidence of substantial harm." Unfortunately, the states are not uniform; that is, they differ in the standard of review used for pulling the religion card into play. So, let us briefly look at the various standards and how they are handled by the courts.

For your further research, the Nolo.com Website succinctly and briefly analyzes the various standards: *www.nolo.com/ lawcenter/ency/article.cfm*. The Nolo.com Website refers to this as the "actual or substantial harm" standard and lists the states that follow this standard: California, Colorado, Florida, Idaho, Indiana, Iowa, Maryland, Massachusetts, Montana, Nebraska, New Jersey, New York, North Dakota, Ohio, Rhode Island, Utah, Vermont, and Washington. For a look at cases that deal with this issue, see *Munoz v. Munoz*, 489 P.2d 1133, 1135; *Pater v. Pater*, 588 N.E.2d 794 (1992); and *In re Murga*, 103 Cal. App. 3rd 498, 163 Cal. Rptr. 79 (1980).

We have already encountered the "clear evidence of substantial harm standard" in the state of Massachusetts through the *Kendall* case. Some states apply a standard that involves only a *risk* of harm.[15] Perhaps one of my favorite cases in the application of this standard is the snake handling case of *Harris v. Harris* (343 S.2d 762 [Miss. 1977]). There, the mother belonged to a Christian denomination that espoused the handling of poisonous snakes as a means of evaluating the condition of ones' soul. The father, concerned over the safety and welfare of his children, sought to remove them from the mother's custody. The court found that there was no evidence of any risk of harm to the children because there was no evidence that the mother had taken the children to services/meetings where the snakes were present. The children remained with the mother.[16] Put another way, the possibility of harm to a child due to a parent's religious beliefs will not negate custody. Some courts still make these decisions on a case by case basis. That is, the courts make their determinations

on the individual facts and circumstances presented without much reference at all to formulas or established equations.

Yeah, great, but I belong to a non-mainstream religion. What does all this mean for me?

The courts have had plenty of practice dealing with non-mainstream
religions. In the case *Gluckstern v. Gluckstern* (158 N.Y.S2d 504, 17
Misc. 83 [1956]), whose litigants were Christian Scientists, the court
took into consideration the parental aversion to modern Western medicine and found that children could be exposed to health risks; children
must have healthcare. When dealing with Jehovah's Witnesses, the court
takes into consideration their aversion to blood transfusions and finds
that children cannot be exposed to health risks; children must have blood
transfusions if they need them. When dealing with religious sects that
practice the handling of poisonous snakes, the court *still* gave the snake
handling parent custody of the children because there had been no showing that the children were exposed to the dangers posed by the snakes.

So, how specifically have the courts dealt with child custody and
Pagan religions? The case law on this topic is somewhat sparse. However,
the case of *Warrick v. Lane* (Texas Court of Appeals, 4th District, San
Antonio, No. 16064 [April 11, 1979]) amply demonstrates the notion
that cries of "The judge took my kids away because I am Wiccan" will
not pass legal muster where there are sufficient other grounds to take the
kids away. Evidence taken at the trial level was quite detailed and included evidence of neglect and unhealthy living conditions while the
children were living with their mother. It should come as no surprise that
the court gave custody of the children to the father. Although the mother
claimed that the trial court violated her constitutional rights under the
Texas and U.S. Constitutions by allowing testimony regarding her religious beliefs and the Church of Wicca, the appellate court dismissed this
assertion by stating that the extensive findings of fact made no reference
to the Church of Wicca or to any other form of religion. There was

enough competent evidence before the trial court to support its ruling without even looking at religion. Clearly, if the courts have a good reason to take your kids away from you without even pulling the religion card, they will do it. In those instances, claims of religious discrimination are not going to be of any avail. If you believe that your religion should not enter into the picture at all, you will need to make a pre-hearing or pre-trial motion to this effect. This is the Motion in Limine that we briefly discussed in Chapter 2.

Then there is the case of *Isbel v. McAbee* (448 So. 2d 372 [Ala. App. 1984]). There, the testimony of the mother and of the father as to their respective parenting abilities differed dramatically. The father alleged that the mother kept a filthy house, kept the children filthy and unsupervised, and tried to heal their sicknesses through witchcraft. The mother's testimony was to the contrary, but the paternal grandparents intervened and alleged that neither parent was fit to raise the children. The mother had given testimony, however, that she had recently taken a job and had relatives to watch her children. As part of its order, the court awarded custody to the mother.

In Michigan, a judge awarded custody of an 8-year-old boy to his mother, who practiced Santeria, complete with animal sacrifice.[17] However, the mother was ordered by the judge not to permit the boy to witness animal sacrifices. It is unknown whether this case was appealed by either the father or the mother.

I HAVE MY KIDS, BUT I DON'T WANT MY EX TO TAKE THEM TO CHURCH. WHAT CAN I DO?

The answer to this question is entirely a matter of state law. In some states, the custodial parent has complete control over religious upbringing.[18] In the case of *Jacobs v. Jacobs* (25 Ill. App. 3rd 175, 323 N.E.2d 21 [1974]), a Jewish father petitioned the court for a modification of an initial child custody decree which had awarded the mother custody. Since the divorce, the mother had converted to Catholicism, had married a Catholic, and had other children, all of whom were being raised

Catholic. This upset the Jewish father of the daughter that the mother had with her Jewish ex-husband. He petitioned the court and claimed that his daughter was being forced to participate in Catholicism, to her detriment. Therefore, he wished to be awarded custody of his daughter.

There are cases that allow the non-custodial parent to expose the children to his/her religious beliefs, even though they are not the religious beliefs of the custodial parent. In the *Munoz* case, a Catholic father was not prohibited from taking his children to Catholic Church services or to Catholic instructional classes even though the mother, who was the custodial parent, was a Mormon. The facts revealed that the children often attended two different religious services on Sundays. The Washington Supreme Court cited the general rule:

> The courts are reluctant, however, to interfere with the religious faith and training of children where the conflicting religious preferences of the parents are in no way detrimental to the welfare of the child. The obvious reason for such a policy of impartiality regarding religious beliefs is that, constitutionally, American courts are forbidden from interfering with religious freedoms or to take steps preferring one religion over another...Thus, the rule appears to be well established that the courts should maintain an attitude of strict impartiality between religions and should not disqualify any applicant for custody or restrain any person having custody or visitation rights from taking the children to a particular church, except where there is a clear and affirmative showing that the conflicting religious beliefs affect the general welfare of the child.

(*Munoz*, 1135)

Following this rule, the court found that there was no affirmative showing in the record indicating that it would be detrimental to the well-being of the children to allow their father to take them to the Catholic Church or to religious instruction in that faith during the periods of his rights of visitation.[19]

Thus, depending on what state you live in, your Pagan children may be exposed to more conventional religious beliefs, or you may expose your non-Pagan children to your religious beliefs even if you are not the custodial parent. Personally, I find that some of these cases read somewhat like the two mothers in the court of King Solomon: the two parents battling for a piece of a child's soul, like the two mothers battle to possess the baby before the King of Judea. Believers in the more orthodox religions may honestly believe that the immortal souls of their children are endangered unless those children are reared within the confines of a certain belief system. I am not aware of any Pagan spiritual tradition that holds such beliefs. It may behoove us, as Pagans, to let our children discover their spirituality on their own. I have known many "recovering Catholics" and "recovering Baptists" who came to Paganism despite rigid religious indoctrination in their natal families. If our children are going to believe as we do, they will come to this on their own, and no amount of religious propagandizing will halt their inevitable arrival at their own spiritual choice. Then again, there are Pagan parents who firmly believe in their rights to indoctrinate/teach their children. Who can say which approach is correct or incorrect? These decisions lie within the family and rightly so. It is not the place of the state to so entangle itself in a child's religious upbringing as to take the place of a parent or a church or Wiccan High Priestess.

THE COURTS MIGHT CUT ME A BREAK, BUT WHAT ABOUT THE DIVISION OF SOCIAL SERVICES, A.K.A. THOSE PEOPLE WHO COME AND TAKE KIDS AWAY?

State agencies that deal with neglected and/or abused children are created by the individual state legislatures and are specifically empowered by them. Thus, to understand the power that such an agency has in your state, you must be familiar with the power given to the agency by your state legislature. Most of what the state agency does is part and parcel of the legislative grant of power to them and is contained in the statutes that govern the agency. This is not a bunch of top secret stuff. Most of these agencies have Websites. Do a search on the Internet for your local office. Additionally, you can probably walk into the local office and obtain pamphlets, leaflets, and other information right out of the front lobby. When I was writing this book, I looked up the Division of Social Services (DSS) in the phone book, found the local office, and called down there to see if they had any informational pamphlets for the public. Yes, they did. I went to the office and picked them up. They were quite informative. You can probably do the same thing.

Regarding Pagans and their fear of having their children removed from their households, what do these agencies do? In immediate terms, the DSS has a system for receiving reports of suspected abuse and neglect. They investigate these reports where serious consequences may result. When a report of suspected abuse/neglect comes in, a social worker is dispatched to the home in order to perform an investigation of that report. Usually, the first thing a Pagan asks is whether a social worker will be dispatched to their home if someone calls in and says: "My daughter-in-law practices witchcraft." This bald statement should not kick off an investigation. Given that Wicca/Witchcraft has been established as a religion meritorious of First Amendment protection, to begin an investigation on such a statement would be analogous to beginning an investigation on the following report: "My daughter-in-law is Catholic, and she let her son be an altar boy." A report like this, however, will probably kick off an investigation: "My daughter-in-law practices witchcraft, and she is going to sacrifice the family dog on Saturday night while the children, ages 5 and 8, watch." Such an embellished report began a chilling investigation in the case of *Wallis v. Spencer*, which will be discussed later in the chapter.

Although this language and case addresses potential establishment clause problems on the part of the judiciary, it is not just the judiciary that must not violate the establishment clauses of the federal and state constitutions: it is the state that cannot do so, and this means all state employees, such as the folks who work at your local DSS office.

Who can make reports? Anyone can make reports. Importantly, the state statutes reveal certain classes of people who are mandated reporters; that is, they are required by law to report cases of abuse/neglect. For example, in Massachusetts, the list of mandated reporters is extensive and includes medical professionals, public and private school teachers, educational administrators, foster parents, firefighters, police officers, and daycare workers.

In Missouri, as well, certain professionals must (and other laypeople may) report cases of abuse or suspected abuse:

> 1. When any physician, medical examiner, coroner, dentist, chiropractor, optometrist, podiatrist, resident, intern, nurse, hospital or clinic personnel that are engaged in the examination, care, treatment or research of persons, and any other health practitioner, psychologist, mental health professional, social worker, day care center worker or other child-care worker, juvenile officer, probation or parole officer, teacher, principal or other school official, Christian Science practitioner, peace officer or law enforcement official, or other person with responsibility for the care of children has reasonable cause to suspect that a child has been or may be subjected to abuse or neglect or observes a child being subjected to conditions or circumstances which would reasonably result in abuse or neglect, that person shall immediately re port or cause a report to be made to the division in accordance with the provisions of sections 210.109 to 210.183. As used in this section, the term "abuse" is not limited to abuse inflicted by a person responsible for the child's care, custody and control as specified in section 210.110, but shall also include abuse inflicted by any other person.
>
> MO.V.A.M.S. Sec. 210.115(1)

Obviously, under the Missouri statute, there must be a report of either past or pending abuse and/or neglect. Again, mere reports that "My son-in-law is a Druid" or "My niece is a Wiccan" are not going to instigate investigations by DSS. A report such as "My niece is a Wiccan, and she does not feed her children anything but saltines and Kool-Aid, and one of the kids had a 103 degree fever last week, and she did nothing," will probably trigger an investigation. What the social workers will be primarily interested in are the reports of suspected malnutrition and lack of appropriate medical care. Once the social worker is in your house, however, and sees your athames and ritual swords in plain view and within easy reach of children, you are going to have some difficulties. This does not necessarily mean you are being persecuted for your religion. Someone leaving a loaded magnum 44 around the house and within easy reach of children is going to have the same difficulties. That does not mean they are being persecuted for being members of the NRA, either. It does mean that there are some open and obvious dangers to children existing in your household that must be addressed.

And what about the people making those reports? They can cause you some significant grief. If you happen to find out who has reported you and if they have said some really heinous and untrue things about you, do you have any options? Again, this depends on the state you are living in. There are some states that take a dim view of false reporting. For example, the Missouri statute provides: "Any person who intentionally files a false report of child abuse or neglect shall be guilty of a class A misdemeanor."[20] Then again, some state statutes repose a certain amount of good faith in the person making the report and offer them a degree of immunity from prosecution.

Just because you are being investigated, does this mean that your children are going to be lifted out of the house? The answer is probably no. Look to the literature supplied by your state agency for the answer but as an example, in the Commonwealth of Massachusetts, DSS asserts that the majority of the children served by the Department will remain in their homes. The goal is to preserve the health and safety needs of children; so, unless the child is at a risk of harm, the Department tries to keep the children in the home. For further research, you can go to your local DSS office and request literature regarding child abuse and neglect.

For example, in Massachusetts, there are two specific publications you may want to read: "Child Abuse and Neglect Reporting: A Guide for Mandated Reporters," September, 2000; and "Child Abuse Hurts Us All: Recognizing, Reporting and Preventing Child Abuse and Neglect," June, 2002. Both were published by the Massachusetts Department of Social Services.

Some people feel utterly powerless in these situations. Again, the literature you can obtain from the agency itself is informative. The Massachusetts literature indicates that after the investigation has occurred, the agency determines whether there was reasonable to believe that abuse or neglect existed. If there is/was reasonable cause, the assessment process begins. If there was no reasonable cause, then there will be no further involvement.[21] The assessment must be completed within 45 days and at that time, there will be an indication of what services are needed. In the state of Massachusetts, this means that a Service Plan is developed by your social workers with the participation of the family/caretakers. You are entitled to disagree with the agency decisions, and you are entitled to a fair hearing to dispute certain decisions or actions taken by DSS or other agencies contracted by it in your case. You must make a written request for the fair hearing within 30 calendar days after receiving notice of the decision with which you disagree.

Finally, what happens if someone within the agency starts making snide comments to you about your religion? What happens if there is something in their behavior or statements, which cause you to believe that your religious beliefs are at issue? If there is anyone in the system who believes that the system protects only mainstream religious families, then you have a real problem. This particular kind of prejudice is insidious and difficult to deal with. I have heard all sorts of horror stories over the years. I have not been able to corroborate most of them, which is a problem. I have heard that Pagans have had to put up with civil servants with attitudes such as "The law only protects Christians," or "You are a Witch; you worship the Devil, and you are never getting these children back!" If such a situation occurs, remember that there are courts that are adamantly opposed to this sort thing. Remember the *Waites* case in Missouri, for example.

Here are some suggestions for dealing with this sort of thing. Always have someone with you when you go to see, speak with, or be interviewed by the Division of Social Services. If, while you are there, a representative with whom you are dealing says something like this to you, then call for a supervisor immediately and do not leave until you get one. If this happens while you have the person in your home, get out a piece of paper and start writing down their reprehensible comments and behavior. Ask for the names of their supervisors. You want to report these occurrences as soon as possible. Once you have the ear of the supervisor, tell her/him what has just occurred in minute detail. If the representative denies it, then the witness you brought along can corroborate your story. There is probably a complaint process, and if so, you may wish to consider filing a formal complaint against the representative immediately. Ask for a new representative to handle your case.

THE *WALLIS* CASE

Woefully, abuses of the system do occur. One particular horror story is illustrated by the case of *Wallis v. Spencer* (202 F.3rd. 1126 [9th Cir. 2000]). In the *Wallis* case, children aged 5 and 2 were removed from a home by city police officers following reports to the San Diego Child Protection Services made by a maternal aunt, who was a hospitalized psychiatric patient. She had made the report to a healthcare professional. Those reports included statements that the parents belonged to a satanic cult; that the father was going to sacrifice his son to Satan at the fall equinox ritual; that there was a cover-up scheme for the contemplated murder; and that the mother might not know what was going to happen. The children were removed from the home and conveyed to a medical hospital where extensive physical examination occurred, including examination of bodily orifices, including vaginal and anal exams. Ultimately, the children were returned to the mother and father, and the juvenile court case was dropped.

As the *Wallis* case painfully points out, once your children are in the hands of the government, it is possible for the government to commit terrible transgressions against them and against you. Procure an attorney immediately and remain ever vigilant in your quest to have the children returned to your custody and discuss your options for a lawsuit if you believe that constitutional infringements against you or your children have occurred.

My soon-to-be ex is threatening to take the kids because I am a Pagan! What do I do?

You married someone who was not a Pagan. You thought they understood. You married someone who was Pagan, and then they were not Pagan anymore. Still, you hoped that they understood. Now, this someone that you used to know, love, and trust wants your kids. This someone is threatening to take them away on the basis of your religion. You are genuinely in a panic. What can you do?

First, start looking for a good lawyer. While you are looking, clean the house, make sure there is nutritious food in the fridge, make sure your kids are clean and are medically well cared for, and if you have any unmarried lovers living with you, make them get a place of their own. There are a number of custody cases where the court took a very dim view of unmarried cohabitation.[22]

Although we covered the "find a lawyer" part in Chapter 1, there are some additional things about the divorce/child custody lawyer that would be helpful to know. These sorts of lawyers usually want a retainer up front; that is, you have to have money to give them at the outset in order for them to represent you. The price will vary widely from lawyer to lawyer and from location to location. There are family law lawyers who want as little as $250 up front, and then there are some who may want a fairly sizeable retainer in the thousands of dollars range.

Do not be intimidated and by all means, do not give up or assume the worst. Remember this: the retainer is something to get started. These types of lawyers usually charge by the hour. After they have used up the retainer, they will begin billing you hourly. Before you pay them any more money after you have given them your retainer, get an itemized bill so that you know what they have been doing on your behalf. Insist on a regular, monthly itemized bill. The lawyer will probably ask you to pay her/him within so many days after receipt of each bill.

You are probably worried about money. Who among us is *not* worried about money? You need to find a way to obtain enough money for a retainer somewhere. Borrow it from your friends, from your family, from your credit card. Go to your community and ask. This is not far-fetched. I know of people who have done it. After all, these are your children, and you could be in for a real fight.

What else can you do? You will have to educate your lawyer. Be familiar with the law in your state pertaining to child custody. Remember that the courts will show an initial reluctance to "judge" religions, but will do so within the context of the state statute relating to child custody as it relates to the "best interests of the child." Religion may not even play a part unless there is a showing of physical or emotional harm caused to the child by pursuing the practices of a certain religion. Finally, all matters heard in court before the judge must be "on the record." This means that they must be recorded by a court reporter and turned into a transcript. Insist on a court reporter and a transcript.

These are your children. Refuse to be bullied or intimidated or frightened. A good parent is a good parent is a good parent, and the courts start from a position of neutrality and impartiality where children are concerned. Do not give them a bona fide reason, such as bad hygiene or poor supervision, to take your children from you.

CHAPTER 5

PAGANS AND EMPLOYMENT DISCRIMINATION

INTRODUCTION

Many Pagans are concerned that their jobs are in jeopardy should anyone find out about their religious beliefs at their places of employment. I have heard a number of complaints over the years: *"Everyone gets to wear their crosses at work, but I can't wear my pentacle." "The born-again Christians are trying to convert me at my job, and I don't know what to do." "My boss made me remove my figurines of the Goddess and the God from the top of my computer monitor, but the Jewish folks get to keep their menorahs, and the Christians get to keep their crosses on their computer monitors." "I took Samhain*

off as a vacation day, someone found out and now, every-
one is making fun of me." And *"I got fired because I am a*
Pagan."

The decision about coming out as a Pagan at work is difficult indeed.[1] Pagans are afraid to come out at work. They are afraid that their
bosses and coworkers are going to find out that they are Pagan and subject them to harassment and humiliation. They are afraid they are going
to get fired. They watch while members of mainstream religions freely
discuss Sunday school or bar mitzvahs at the water cooler, but feel that
they cannot discuss Wiccanings, handfastings, or the ritual they held on
the last Sabbat. Some Pagans claim that they have been targeted by zeal-
ous coworkers who aggressively try to convert them and make it difficult
to perform a job. What can these people do?

Pagans have the protection of state and federal law

There are well-established federal and state laws that protect you from
these sorts of practices. These laws establish that employees that have a
"right to work in an environment free from discriminatory intimidation,
ridicule, and insult."[2] By means of a federal statute, the United States
Congress has "provided the courts with a means to preserve religious
diversity from forced religious conformity."[3] The state legislatures have
taken similar action by enacting corresponding state statutes. The state
statutes are written differently from state to state and therefore, you must
check the applicable employment discrimination statute in your state if
you wish to file any charges under it.

To learn more about them, all you have to do is go online and examine the Website for the applicable federal agency, which is the Equal Employment Opportunity Commission (EEOC), *www.eeoc.gov.* There will
be a corresponding state agency to address your state's anti-discrimination laws, and they will have a Website as well. The EEOC has a page of

questions and answers that should answer many of the questions that lay people have about on-the-job discrimination. Please refer to *www.eeoc.gov/facts/qanda.html*. Follow the links on the state Websites for similar FAQs.

For those of us who still love books and libraries, there are some very good books addressing this area of the law. A good book for laypeople is *Job Discrimination II: How to Fight, How to Win!*, by Jeffrey M. Bernbach, Esq. For an excellent compilation of cases and references to other legal resources, see 149 A.L. R. Fed. 405 (2001): ANNOTATION: "What Constitutes Religious Harassment in Employment in Violation of Title VII of Civil Rights Act of 1964," by David J. Stephenson, Jr., J.D., Ph.D.

SO, WHAT ARE PAGANS AFRAID OF?

Pagans should take heart. The Pagan road to recognition and compensation is being paved. There are Pagans out there who have taken their grievances to the system and have fared quite well.[4] The problem that most Pagans struggle with in a case of job-related religious discrimination or harassment is actually standing up for themselves, which will mean coming out of the broom closet and being aggressive in the pursuit of their rights. This is an understandable fear. Many are afraid to take a stand because they do not understand exactly what those rights are. Even folks who are reasonably confident about their rights are still reluctant to stand up for them because they are afraid that they will be targeted and fired. Who can afford to be fired? And who can afford a lawyer when they are out of work? Acts of retaliation by an employer against an employee such as these are illegal, and there are Websites devoted to providing affordable legal representation in the area of discrimination. For example, see Legal Fairness for All, located at *www.legalfairnessforall.com/discrimination-goo.htm*.

Standing up for the right to work in an environment free from religious discrimination is a decision which, ultimately, only the individual can make. It may eventually involve some very real logistical problems, like getting fired. In order to make a case for religious discrimination in the workplace, you must put the employer on notice that it is occurring and that the workplace has, indeed, become hostile. If we are talking about coworkers who are harassing you, then you must tell your supervisor that it is occurring. If we are talking about a supervisor who is making your life difficult or not responding to your grievances, then you may need to take your complaints to his/her higher up, but someone in a position of authority must know that because of your religious convictions you are being harassed and that consequently, your work environment has become hostile.

You should know...

If you were supplied with a company manual when you were hired, read it thoroughly. There may be a section that tells you exactly what you are supposed to do if you experience harassment on the job. Manuals to training programs provided by a company to its employees and managerial trainees will probably address all forms of harassment contemplated under Title VII. The manual will probably set forth an entire procedure for dealing with claims of harassment that are in violation of the anti-discrimination laws. A manager or supervisor who does not comply with the manuals for whom he/she works could be fired by that company. The manual may discuss definitions of the "reasonable accommodations" that an employer is supposed to make on the basis of religion and may also discuss the notion of disparate treatment; that is, the intentional and different treatment of an employee based on protected status, such as religion. Importantly, please note that "reasonable accommodation" is not required if it would impose an "undue hardship" on the business. New employees should request a copy of their job description, as well as copies of any manuals or other literature that explains their job, what is expected of them, how they should dress, what accessories they may wear, etc. For example, there may be a section on employee appearance, and it may even contain a discussion of appropriate jewelry for the employee.

As a practical matter, there should be some sort of paper trail indicating that you have put your employer on notice. The paper trail is an important aspect of the case. Defense counsel for labor relations cases typically review all documents relating to a complainant. You will probably need to place a letter or memorandum in your file to this effect. Keep a copy for yourself. It might also be helpful if you keep a journal of all the harassment: the dates, times, and places that they occurred, who committed them, and the particulars of the harassment, such as what was said or done. Log any other gruesome details.

How important are such things as clothing and accessories? Carol Grotts, a Pentecostal Christian, sued Brinks, the armored car company, over their requirement that she wear pants. According to Ms. Grotts, her religion did not permit her to wear pants, and she offered to pay for a similar alternative garment. In the resulting legal struggle, she won a $30,000 legal settlement.[5] In the same article as cited previously, Wiccan postal worker Robert Hurston discussed the difficulties he faced when he wore a "Born Again Pagan" T-shirt while coworkers wearing crucifixes or clothes with Christian images "never drew a second look."[6]

However, once you have done all this, you may very well become a target for firing. This means that the employer may find some reason to fire you, such as frequent tardiness, too many days missed from work, work that is poorly done, or any other excuse. After all, one of the best defenses to a cause of action for discriminatory discharge is that the employer had a bona fide reason to fire you in the first place. One of the tricks to successfully defending such an allegation from your employer is to be a good employee: dress appropriately for the job; get to work on time; do the job assigned to you; make an effort to get along with your coworkers; and miss work only for legitimate reasons, such as illness.

Employers will produce your personnel file, and your entire work history will be exposed in court. If you have been a bad employee, it is going to be out there for the whole world to see. For example, in the case of *Lynch v. Pathmark Supermarkets* (987 F. Supp. 236 [D.C.S.N.Y. 1997]), Plaintiff was a born-again Christian who alleged that he was terminated due to religious discrimination. Even though some coworkers had made some questionable remarks about Plaintiff's religion, the court found that there was ample evidence to support the termination of Plaintiff's employment based on absenteeism, poor work performance, antagonism with coworkers, use of profanity, excessive lateness, theft, and fighting with coworkers.[7]

Similarly, if you have a good work record, that record will also come to light. In the case *Young v. Southwestern Savings and Loan Ass'n.* (509 F. 2d 140 [5th Cir. 1975]), an atheist with an excellent work record resigned after being told that business meetings that opened with prayer and religious commentary were mandatory and that she must attend the meetings from beginning to end. In the case of *Goldberg v. City of Philadelphia, et al.* (65 Empl. Prac. Dec. P 43,221 [1994]), a Jewish police officer refuted Defendants' allegations of poor work performance with 11 years' worth of glowing personnel evaluation reports.

You should be especially aware of two things. First, an employer is required to reasonably accommodate an employee's religious belief, or that of a prospective employee, unless doing so would impose an undue hardship. This would appear to have been the gravamen of a Pentecostal Christian's complaint with her employer when she offered to pay for a similar uniform, without pants. Second, if reasonable accommodation occurs, the employer may be off the hook. Third, your rights should be no big secret, as employers are required to post notices to all employees that advise them of their rights under the laws that the EEOC enforces and their right to be free from retaliation. For more information about reasonable accommodation and applicable rights, see *www.eeoc.gov/facts/qanda.html.*[8]

Believe it or not, a lot of people with some wide-ranging religious beliefs have pursued relief for employment discrimination based on religion. The courts have dealt with atheists (as in the *Young* case), Jews (as in the *Goldberg* case), Cambodian Buddhists (in the case of *Sarin v. Raytheon*) fundamentalist Christian sects (*Blalock v. Metals Trades, Inc.*), and yes, even Pagans—as in the *Henderson, Dodge,* and *Van Koten* cases, which we'll be looking at shortly. The bottom line here is that Wiccans have already filed employment discrimination claims and have been successful. These cases are significant legal landmarks for Pagans.

WHAT IS THE BASIS FOR MY RIGHT TO WORK IN A DISCRIMINATION-FREE ENVIRONMENT?

First, there are no provisions or clauses in the Federal Constitution that address religious discrimination at the job outright. As is true for most questions regarding the states, you will have to check the constitution in your state to see if they are any clauses in it that directly address religious discrimination and employment. A state-based cause of action for discrimination in employment practices may arise exclusively under a state's statute. For example, in the Commonwealth of Massachusetts, the court held in the case *Quercia v. Allmerica Financial* (84 F. Supp. 2d, 228 [D. Mass. 2000]) that the anti-discrimination statute is the exclusive remedy for employment discrimination complaint.

Please check with a competent local attorney specializing in employment discrimination to determine where you are able to file claims for damages regarding both federal claims under Title VII and under your state's anti-discrimination statutes. Your religious discrimination claim may have other aspects other than those derived from religion. For example, there may be a physical handicap component to it. In that event, you could have a concomitant claim under the Americans with Disabilities Act of 1992 (often referred to as the ADA). In the case of Wiccan postal worker Mr. Hurston, he had a hearing loss for which he was taunted, and this accompanied his claim of religious harassment arising out of his Wiccan-based religious beliefs.

The basis for a federal claim of religious discrimination in employment arises under Title VII of the Civil Rights Act of 1964 (42 U.S.C.A. Sections 2000e, *et seq.*). The statute sets forth unlawful employment practices as follows:

> It shall be an unlawful employment practice for an employer—(1) to fail or refuse to hire or to discharge any individual, or otherwise to discriminate against any individual with respect to his compensation, terms, conditions, or privileges of employment, because of such individual's race, color, religion, sex, or national origin; or (2) to limit, segregate, or classify his employees or applicants for employment in any way which would deprive or tend to deprive any individual of employment opportunities or otherwise adversely affect his status as an employee, because of such individual's race, color, religion, sex, or national origin.

> 42 U.S.C.A. Sections 2000e-2(a)(1)-(2)

The federal statute Title VII addresses businesses with more than 25 employees. The EEOC Website has a question and answer page (*www.eeoc.gov/facts/qanda.html*) regarding the federal laws that prohibit discrimination and sets forth the discriminatory practices under them. As we have already seen, states have corresponding statutes providing a state-based cause of action for discrimination in the work place.

Many Pagans throw up their hands and say: *"Yes, this is great, but my employer does not think that what I do or believe is a religion and therefore, they are not illegally discriminating against me."* In some ways, this brings us back to our discussion in Chapter 3 about how "religion" is defined. However, the federal statute defines religion as follows:

The term 'religion' includes all aspects of religious observance and practice, as well as belief, unless an employer
demonstrates that he is unable to reasonably accommodate to an employee's or prospective employee's religious
observance or practice without undue hardship on the
conduct of the employer's business.

42 U.S.C.A. Section 2000e(j)

There are supporting regulations that further define a religion for
purposes of Title VII. See C.F.R. Section 1605.1, which states that a
religion may include "moral or ethical beliefs as to what is right and
wrong which are sincerely held with the strength of traditional religious
views...The fact that no religious group espouses such beliefs or the fact
that the religious group to which the individual professes to belong may
not accept such belief will not determine whether the belief is a religious
belief of the employee..." In the case *Van Koten v. Family Health Management, Inc.* (955 F. Supp. 898 [1997], *aff'd,* 134 F.3rd 375 [7th Cir.
1998]) the Seventh Circuit Court of Appeals looked to all this language
in determining whether Wiccan practitioner Dr. Van Koten held religious beliefs that merited the protection of Title VII. Even though the
Plaintiff in the Van Koten case did not win the overall war, he did win
the battle on whether Wicca was a religion for the purposes of Title VII
protection. The court went on to use some language which should, by
now, be quite familiar to us. The test to be used in order to determine
what is a "religion" for the purposes of Title VII is whether the belief for
which protection is sought is religious in the person's own scheme of
things and whether that belief is sincerely held.

WHERE CAN I TAKE MY PROBLEM?

There are several possible venues for filing an action against your
employer based on religious discrimination. Federal claims raised under
Title VII may be filed with the EEOC. Before you can proceed to a
private lawsuit, the Title VII charges of discrimination must be filed
with the EEOC. Again, be sure to look at *www.eeoc.gov/facts/qanda.html.*

After you have filed with the EEOC and have followed all the correct procedures, the federal courts may be available to you. Similarly, claims based on a state's anti-discrimination laws may be filed in one of the state or local agencies. After you have filed your state claim in the appropriate state agency, the state courts may be available to you.

However, there are some restrictions on both agency and court filings that you should be aware of. Before you file anything, it might be wise to contact the EEOC, your state agency, and your attorney so that when you do file, you file the right thing in the right place at the right time.

What do I have to prove?

This is the nitty-gritty of a discrimination case, as it is the nitty-gritty of any legal proceeding. There are several different kinds of employment discrimination cases: the hostile work environment case, the disparate treatment case, the constructive discharge case, the wrongful discharge case, the retaliatory discharge case, and the *quid pro quo* harassment case. We are going to look at most of these scenarios, but the only treatment of the *quid pro quo* case will be this: in that sort of case, the supervisor will usually demand that an employee alter or renounce some religious belief in exchange for job benefits. See the case *Weiss v. U.S.* (595 F. Supp. 1050 [D.C. Va. 1984]) for illustration.

The hostile work environment case

Does the employee have to wait until a nervous breakdown, or something similar, occurs before treatment on the job becomes actionable? No. Actionable treatment on the job will create a hostile work environment or one that is intimidating or offensive. The treatment complained of will have, as its purpose or effect, the consequence of unreasonably interfering with an individual's work performance. Basically, Plaintiff will need to show that the conduct was rerious, repetitive, and habitual. Isolated or occasional conduct/comments or merely offensive utterances are not going to pass muster.

The burden of proof initially carried by the Plaintiff will probably include a showing such as the following:

> 1) unwelcome comments, jokes, acts, and other verbal or physical conduct of an ethnic and/or religious nature made in the workplace; 2) such conduct had the effect of creating an intimidating, hostile, or offensive working environment, or unreasonably interfered with an individual's work performance; and 3) the employer knew or should have known of the conduct.

> (*Sarin*, 52)

To contrast, the federal district court in Pennsylvania in the *Goldberg* case stated:

> To demonstrate the existence of a hostile environment, [Plaintiff] must establish...(1) the employee suffered intentional discrimination because of his religion; (2) the discrimination was pervasive and regular; (3) the discrimination detrimentally affected the plaintiff; (4) the discrimination would detrimentally affect a reasonable person of the same religion in that position; and (5) the existence of respondeat superior liability.

> (*Goldberg*, Lexis 10)

What sort of conduct has passed muster or risen to the level of actionable conduct? In the *Goldberg* case, a Jewish Philadelphia policeman was subjected to considerable verbal abuse. You can see it for yourself on pages 2–3 of the case print out from the Lexis service. There were also incidents of physical violence. For example, one coworker choked Mr. Goldberg around the neck for several seconds. Mr. Goldberg claimed that he received death threats, his phone calls were interrupted, the materials on his desk were pushed around, and trash was delivered to his home. Mr. Goldberg was transferred from one unit to another but still, the abuse continued and finally, he was moved from a plainclothes work unit to a uniform patrol job, which he perceived as a demotion. Regarding this veritable crusade against the Plaintiff Goldberg, the court found that the incidents were repeated, pervasive, and regular. They were discriminatory and based on his religion. Plaintiff also showed that this conduct affected him such that he was forced to resign. This conduct would have detrimentally affected a reasonable Jewish person, and thus, Plaintiff had established his *prima facie* case.

There is an important aspect to these cases about which potential Plaintiffs should be aware: Actions taken by the employer to counteract the discriminatory working conditions may be sufficient to defeat liability under a discrimination claim. If, upon learning of the discriminatory treatment, the employer takes immediate, corrective action, the employer may be absolved of liability. In *Sarin v. Raytheon* (905 F. Supp. 49 [D.C.Mass. 1995]), the *Sarin* court noted that under Title VII, an employer's remedial actions can effectively shield the employer from liability for harassment committed by a supervisor. In the *Sarin* case, the Plaintiff was a Cambodian Buddhist harassed by coworkers on the job. Disciplinary action was taken against the coworkers, and they received reprimands. A hearing also occurred. The coworkers were required to apologize, and at least one of them was moved to another station. The harassment ended. Offers to move Plaintiff to a different site away from the culprits were also made. However, Plaintiff declined these.

THE DISPARATE TREATMENT CASE

Regarding disparate treatment, a white Jewish deputy in the U.S. Marshal's Service in Washington, D.C., filed a Title VII claim in the case of *Turner v. Barr* (806 F. Supp. 1025, 65 Fair Empl. Prac. Cas. [BNA] 904, 61 Emp. Prac. Dec. [CCH] P42, 090 [D.D.C. 1992]). There, the Plaintiff worked with many black coworkers. The white deputies were referred to as "white asses" and "white boys." The white deputies were huddled in the back of the room. Plaintiff asserted that one black deputy told Plaintiff "to get his 'white ass out of the office' because 'this is a black office, for blacks, supervised by blacks.'"[9]

Importantly, Plaintiff was treated differently from other workers regarding an escaped prisoner. Plaintiff was not interviewed until 10 months after the incident. He was not given an opportunity to review what had occurred before being interviewed. The final report was riddled with errors and showed a clear lack of regard for detail and precision. The Investigator admitted that he failed to investigate a number of other relevant matters. Plaintiff was disciplined regarding this event; however, a black coworker who was also involved received only a "letter of instruction." This letter was not disciplinary in nature and did not go down in the coworker's permanent record. The court specifically found that the Plaintiff was singled out for discipline and was working in a repressive atmosphere where his race and religion were at issue. There was sufficient evidence to pervasive harassment such that a hostile, offensive work environment existed. Plaintiff had proven his Title VII case.

THE CONSTRUCTIVE DISCHARGE CASE

What is constructive discharge? Essentially, constructive discharge occurs when the working conditions have become so difficult that the employee is compelled to leave the job. In *Young v. Southwestern Sav. and Loan Ass'n.* (409 F.2d 140 [5th Cir. 1995]), an example of constructive discharge, an atheist employed as a teller in a Texas savings and loan institution objected to activities at mandatory staff meetings. Those activities included religious talk and prayer. On one occasion, the devotionals were delivered by a local Baptist minister and on another occasion by a Protestant cleric. The branch manager of Plaintiff's office told Plaintiff that the meetings were mandatory in their entirety and as for her religious objections, Plaintiff could simply " 'close her ears.' "[10] Thereafter, Plaintiff resigned and later filed suit. The court found that this was "precisely the situation in which the doctrine of constructive discharge applies, a case in which an employee involuntarily resigns in order to escape intolerable and illegal employment requirements."[11]

THE RETALIATORY DISCHARGE CASE

The *Weiss* case is instructive for looking at retaliatory discharge. There, Plaintiff was a Jewish employee, and for two years, he was subjected to anti-Semitic comments. Plaintiff was taunted by such remarks as " 'resident Jew,' " " 'Jew faggot,' " " 'rich Jew,' " " 'Christ killer,' " " 'nail him to the cross,' " and " 'you killed Christ...so you'll have to hang from the cross.' " [12] Obviously, Pagans have no corner on the market when it comes to being called rude, crass, and highly offensive names.

Plaintiff did not report or complain about this conduct, but he did develop stress- and anxiety-related disorders as a consequence of this conduct. At this point, the supervisor took action against the coworker, but did not fire the coworker. Unhappy with the action taken by the supervisor, Plaintiff complained to the supervisor's higher up. This higher up generally supported the disciplinary action taken by the supervisor. The supervisor figured out that Plaintiff had complained about him (the supervisor) and began to take retaliatory action against Plaintiff: The supervisor gave Plaintiff inappropriate and unreasonably difficult work assignments; rated Plaintiff's work performance substantially lower than prior to Plaintiff's complaints; and often berated and demeaned Plaintiff in front of others. Generally, however, Plaintiff had received high performance evaluations and had worked to his supervisors' satisfaction.

On May 18, 1982, Plaintiff initiated EEO counseling and named his supervisor as the Alleged Discriminating Official. After being questioned by the EEO counselor, the supervisor threatened to sue Plaintiff. The supervisor and Plaintiff continued to be at odds with one another, but the supervisor began bringing groundless disciplinary actions against the Plaintiff. Finally, Plaintiff's third line supervisor fired Plaintiff on the supervisor's proposal. The agency for whom all these people worked never disciplined the supervisor for his conduct; yet, Plaintiff developed headaches, stomach pains, nausea, and bleeding and cracking on his hands. All in all, Plaintiff's work performance and conduct in the office suffered. The agency for which they all worked refused to reassign the Plaintiff to another branch.

The court stated that Plaintiff had a right to non-discriminatory terms and conditions of employment; that Plaintiff's opposition to abuse was protected by Title VII; and that Plaintiff's participation in EEO proceedings was similarly protected. The court noted that in order to make out a case of retaliatory discharge, the Plaintiff had to show that he opposed an employment practice which was unlawful under Title VII, that he was subsequently subjected to an adverse employment action, and that there was a causal connection between the two. The court specifically found that the Defendants attempted to justify Plaintiff's discharge on the premise of poor work performance and further, that this reason was "merely a pretext, developed by [the] supervisor...for the underlying motivation to fire Mr. Weiss for his charges of discrimination against [the supervisor]."[13]

In this case, the employment agency was among the named Defendants. To hold the employer liable, Plaintiff needed to "establish that the employer had actual or constructive knowledge of the existence of the offensive discriminatory or retaliatory working environment and yet took no prompt and adequate remedial action."[14] Where Plaintiff could prove that he lodged complaints with the employer or that the harassment endured was pervasive, the awareness of the employer could be inferred. The court rendered judgment in favor of the Plaintiff regarding Title VII violations of work discrimination due to religion and national ancestry.

THERE ARE PROCEDURAL POINTS
THAT MUST BE FOLLOWED

Frankly, presenting the substance of your discrimination claim might not be the toughest thing you deal with. There are some tricky aspects to the employment discrimination case of which you should be aware. The first is the Statute of Limitations. The Statute of Limitations sets a time limit for bringing your employment discrimination matter. If you fail to file your claim in the appropriate place within the appropriate time, then the game is over. This means that no matter how great your case is, you blew the time limitations, and you have lost your right to sue over it. See Attorney Bernbach's book, listed in the bibliography, for a more in-depth discussion of the where's and when's to file your claim.

Title VII sets forth the time limitation as follows:

> A charge under this section shall be filed within one hundred and eighty days after the alleged unlawful employment practice occurred and notice of the charge (including the date, place and circumstances of the alleged unlawful employment practice: shall be served upon the person against whom such charge is made within ten days thereafter, except that in a case of an unlawful employment practice with respect to which the person aggrieved has initially instituted proceedings with a State or local agency with authority to grant or seek relief from such practice or to institute criminal proceedings with respect thereto upon receiving notice thereof, such charge shall be filed by or on behalf of the person aggrieved within three hundred days after the alleged unlawful employment practice occurred, or within thirty days after receiving notice that the State or local agency has terminate the proceedings under the State or local law, whichever is earlier, and a copy of such charge shall be filed by the Commission with the State or local agency.

> 42 U.S.C.A. Section 2000e-5(e)(1)

Although 180 days is roughly six months, that is just not a lot of time. It sounds like a lot of time, but taken with everything else that confronts human beings living in the 21st century, it is easy to lose track of time. The notion of "Pagan Standard Time" does not apply where legal proceedings and the protection of your rights are concerned, so don't sit around waiting for something to happen.

In addition to timely filing deadlines, there is the issue of where you must file. Sometimes, these two issues go hand in hand. For example, if you ultimately wish to pursue a Title VII action in federal court, then you must file your claim with the EEOC first, and you must do so within the applicable time limitation. You cannot sue in federal court unless you have first filed with the EEOC. There are some real reasons for preferring to file a discrimination matter in federal court. For example, federal judges are part of the federal court system, and they are not part of the state or local government scene. Thus, a federal judge is less likely to be part of any perceived local nepotism or localized prejudice.

At its Website, the EEOC cautions that in order to protect your rights, the EEOC should be contacted promptly when discrimination is suspected, and that you must file within 180 days from the date of the alleged violation. After having filed with the EEOC, you cannot proceed to federal court until after the agency has issued a Right to Sue Letter. The Right to Sue Letter is issued by the EEOC and puts you on notice that the involvement of the EEOC with your claim is over, which is why you now have a right to sue in federal court. Just to be sure that you protect your claim, it is probably a good idea to start calculating your 90 days from the date listed on the letter, not from the date that you receive it. Again, 90 days sounds like a lot of time, but really, it is not.

Where do you go to file your claim with the EEOC? Where are its offices? Check the EEOC Website, *www/ eeoc.gov*, which has a listing of offices. For filing a state claim, check the Website for the state agency.

Similarly, for actions brought under state anti-discrimination laws, the state agency is the door through which you enter the state court. If you wish to file a suit in state court for your state claim, you must first file in the applicable state agency. You must check your state statute in order to determine the time frame within which you can file your claim in the state agency. Usually, that time frame is longer in the state agency than it is in the EEOC. Sometimes it is as long as 300 days from notice of the alleged discriminatory act. However, you must check your state statute to be sure of the exact time limitation. Again, this sounds like a lot of time, but it is not. Once in the state agency, you usually cannot bring the discrimination claim in state court until the state agency issues the Right to Sue Letter, and then, you may have less than 90 days to bring your action in state court.

Thus, you have two Statutes of Limitation you must comply with if you are going to file suit in the federal or in the state court: the initial time for filing with the agency and the time for filing in the court after you have received your Right to Sue Letter from the agency you filed with in the first place. This entire process is the exhaustion of administrative remedies. One of the first places that defense counsel will look when defending the employer is whether the complaining employee has met all the procedural prerequisites. Unless you follow these procedures, your federal court claim could be dismissed outright. Unless you follow the procedures outlined by your state statutes, your state anti-discrimination claim could be dismissed outright, as well. This happened to the state-based discrimination claims of the Jewish policeman in the *Goldberg* case. His state anti-discrimination claims were dismissed.

Does all this sound complicated? Well, it is, and these are exactly the reasons why you should obtain the services of a lawyer, for navigation of these waters. If your lawyer blows your Statute of Limitations, then your avenue of redress is to sue the lawyer for legal malpractice.

LET'S REVIEW SOME PAGAN-SPECIFIC CASES

One particularly interesting case dealing with Wicca is that of Jamie Dodge, *Dodge v. Salvation Army* (1989 WL 3857 [S.D. Miss.] 48 Empl. Prac. Dec. P38, 619 [1989]). This case is also an example of wrongful discharge. Plaintiff initially filed her claim with the EEOC, but the matter eventually came before the United States District Court for the Southern District of Mississippi, southern division. Plaintiff was employed by the Salvation Army in its Domestic Violence Shelter as the Victim's

Assistance Coordinator. A review of the facts by the court revealed that the Salvation Army was a church, operating as a religious corporation.

So, what happened? One day, Plaintiff was at the copy machine, and she confessed to the Director of the Domestic Violence Shelter that she was using the copy machine to reproduce manuals and information relating to what she described as Satanic/Wiccan rituals. Plaintiff was fired shortly thereafter. Her termination letter advised that she had admitted to copying material that was inconsistent with the religious purposes of her employer. The court noted that Plaintiff was obviously fired for what she believed and what she was copying; she was not fired for the mere act of copying.

The court analyzed this case under the *Lemon* test we discussed in Chapter 3. The court had to contend with the complex issue of funding: What was the source of the grants paying Plaintiff's salary? This was crucial because, if the funds came from government rather than a religious organization, then the issue was one of government entanglement with religion. Plaintiff's job was funded by federal, state, and local government. As such, the religious exemption under which the Salvation Army might have, indeed, been able to discriminatorily treat Plaintiff did not come into play; that is, the religious exemption entitling the Salvation Army to exemption from Title VII anti-discrimination employment practices was not available to the Salvation Army as a defense for its actions. Straining the facts through the *Lemon* test, the court ruled that in this situation, the grants came from the government. Therefore, the Salvation Army could not discriminate against Plaintiff due to her religion. To do otherwise would be a violation of the Establishment Clause, having a primary effect of advancing religion and creating excessive government entanglement. Thus, Plaintiff's case survived a pre-trial attempt by the Defendants to have it dismissed.

The equation of Wicca with Satanism in this case is somewhat troubling as nearly every Wiccan I know vehemently denies that Wicca has anything to do with Satanism. Most Satanists would probably agree. It is important to note that here, the equation of Satanism with Wicca was made by the court based on the evidence presented, which included an article written in a magazine by Plaintiff. There, Plaintiff confessed that she had been misled by Satan and that Wiccans had erroneously convinced her that witchcraft was not Satanism. It would appear that at some point, Plaintiff had been a practicing Wiccan but had later come to believe that her Wiccan/Pagan/witchcraft beliefs were Satanically based. The court used this article, written by the Plaintiff herself, to equate Wicca with Satanism. Now, as troubling as this might appear to be at first glance, it is actually somewhat heartening. The case could be used for the proposition that even if Wicca is Satanically based, it does not matter for the purposes of constitutional review and probably for the purposes of Title VII review, as well, since this was obviously a Title VII case, having first been filed with the EEOC. This would indicate that even belief systems involving the deification of Satan are entitled to protection under both the Constitution and Title VII.

The *Van Koten* case

In the *Van Koten* case, Plaintiff was a chiropractor on hire by the defendant Family Health Management (FMH), but leased out to the Defendant Chiromed Physicians, P.C. (Chiromed). Dr. Van Koten was a practicing Wiccan, and he claimed that he was fired based on his religious beliefs. Dr. Van Koten's Title VII case was heard before a federal magistrate, but the case never went to a full hearing or trial. Defendants filed a pre-trial Motion for Summary Judgement that the magistrate decided in favor of the Defendants. Thus, the case was dismissed before it ever got to a full hearing. The magistrate essentially determined, prior to trial, that Plaintiff had failed to establish one crucial element of his case: that when the defendants fired the Plaintiff, they knew that he was a Wiccan. Plaintiff had established all other elements of his case, including the fact that Wicca was a religion for the purposes of Title VII. Based upon the evidence presented, the magistrate concluded that Wicca "may be considered a Title VII 'religion.' "[15]

In order for Dr. Van Koten's firing to be discriminatory, the Defendants had to know about his religion, and the Defendants proved to the satisfaction of the court that they did not know Dr. Van Koten was a Wiccan. In examining whether the Defendants had knowledge of the fact that Dr. Van Koten was a Wiccan, the doctor did not fare so well. Hence, his termination was not discriminatory in nature. In reading the case, there is nothing in it which shows that Dr. Van Koten had told either his coworkers or his supervisors that he was a Wiccan, that Wicca was a religion, and/or that he was a practicing Wiccan. Having failed to prove that the Defendants knew he was a member of the religion known as Wicca, Dr. Van Koten lost his case on a pre-trial motion. In this respect, he fared less well than did Jamie Dodge in her case. This case, like *Dodge, Dettmer,* and *Ravenwood,* reinforces the caveat that evidence is essential when Pagans attempt to prove that what they practice and believe is, indeed, a religion.

What does this say to Pagans about coming out of the "broom closet" at work? It says that if you are going to claim that you have been treated in a discriminatory fashion because of your religious beliefs, then you are going to have to show that someone did, indeed, know about your religious beliefs. If you are going to claim that you were fired or treated poorly because you are a Wiccan, a Druid, a member of the Asatrú, etc., then you are going to have to prove that your employer knew that you were one of these Pagan spiritual traditions.

THE *HURSTON* CASE

Finally, there is the case of *Hurston v. Henderson* (2001 WL 65202 [E.E.O.C.]) which involved Robert Hurston, an electronic technician at the St. Paul, Minnesota, U.S. Postal office. Mr. Hurston had hearing loss, which brought him within the purview of the Rehabilitation Act,[16] and this statute prohibits discrimination on the basis of a disability. He was also a practicing Wiccan, which brought him within the purview of Title VII.

Mr. Hurston claimed that he was treated differently from other workers. He was not allowed to wear his religious shirts or his religious jewelry. He was also not allowed to display a small cauldron on the job. Mr. Hurston complained that members of other religions were not restricted in the display of their religious symbols and messages; they were not warned about offending others. The Administrative Law Judge (ALJ) examined the evidence and found that the agency supervisor told Mr. Hurston "not to be so open about his religious beliefs."[17] The ALJ also found that Mr. Hurston's coworkers openly chastised him about his religious expression. Mr. Hurston was repeatedly warned about wearing his religious T-shirts, while other employees were permitted to express Christian or Jewish themes on their clothing. The supervisor told Mr. Hurston that he could not wear a pentagram at work; meantime, coworkers were allowed to wear crucifixes, crosses, and Stars of David.

The ALJ found that discriminatory harassment based on religion existed. The actions of the coworkers and the actions of management, together with the failure of management to put a halt to the harassment, created a hostile work environment for Mr. Hurston. The EEOC specifically stated: "...the agency permitted complainant's coworkers to subject him to a barrage of humiliating comments and that management unreasonably restricted complainant's personal religious expression. We further find that the treatment created an humiliating, intimidating, hostile, and offensive work environment."[18] The agency was found liable for harassment.

What do these cases mean for Pagans on the job? First, most Pagan spiritual traditions, especially those that are deity-specific, will pass muster on the "is what you practice and believe a religion" question if the right evidence is presented. Without question, Wicca passes muster. Witches who profess belief in deities, and who live according to some sort of ethical code, will also probably pass muster, but again, look to your evidence! Second, Pagan spiritual traditions are protected by the federal and state anti-discrimination laws. So, all the protection afforded to Catholics, Jews, Protestants, etc., should also be afforded to Pagans; that is, Pagans cannot be fired just because they are Pagans, and they cannot be treated differently from everyone else. If Joe Catholic gets to wear his crucifix and if Sarah Hebrew gets to wear her Star of David, then Carol Rising Moon Wiccan gets to wear her pentacle and Bob Tall Oak Druid gets to wear his Green Man T-shirt. If your Jewish neighbor a few cubicles down can display his menorah on his desk and if your

Catholic friends can display their crucifixes, then the Pagan employees can put up cauldrons and display their deities.

GREAT, BUT WHAT AM I ENTITLED TO?

Under the federal statute, there is a wide range of damages potentially available. Recoverable damages for Title VII actions involving religious harassment include compensatory damages for emotional distress, humiliation, and mental anguish (awarded for effects on your health), punitive damages (designed to punish the employer and act as a deterrent against similar conduct in the future), and attorney's fees. Thus, you have a potential card up your sleeve when going to visit an attorney and asking that attorney to take your case. If your case is good, the defendant may have to pay your lawyer and not you.

See 149 A.L.R. Fed. 405. This Annotation lists other possible forms of recovery, depending on the facts presented by your case: unfair trade practices, assault, battery, false imprisonment, breach of contract, slander, libel, section 1983 or section 1985 civil rights claims, wrongful termination or constructive wrongful termination, and violation of state labor statutes.

In addition to your attorney fees if you win, your opponent may have to pay the other costs of your litigation. Other damages that may be available are back pay, future pay, and reinstatement. Always discuss your possible remedies, forms of redress, and damages with your attorney. You want to be sure that you get everything you are entitled to. You may also be entitled to recover under various tort theories: intentional infliction of emotional distress or the negligent infliction of emotional distress. Courts have enjoined the employer and the employer's agents, servants, and employees from making slurs contrary to their fellow employee's religious beliefs. In the *Turner* case, the court ordered that the reprimand which the employee received be expunged from his record.

As you can see, the employment problems that many Pagans fear have been faced by others, and a substantial body of law has arisen out of their problems. Critical issues will be the establishment of what you believe as a religion and the notice given to your employer that you are being harassed. If you have any doubts as to whether what you are experiencing is harassment or is actionable under the law, consult with an attorney, even if you are incurring an out-of-pocket expense or an hourly consultation fee. The resulting peace of mind could be well worth it.

Do you have to take it?

As the foregoing discussion demonstrates, if you are the victim of pervasive and continuous abuse at work due to your religion, you do not have to stand for it. However, there is probably no way you can continue to remain in the closet and receive either remedial action or redress for what is happening to you. For most Pagans, the initial decision as to whether they should be "out" at work will probably be the hardest, but be of stout heart. These trails already have footprints on them.

CHAPTER 6

PAGANS AND THE RENT

INTRODUCTION

In addition to worries about losing their children and/or their jobs, many Pagans fear the loss of their homes due to religious discrimination. It is a frightening thought: that a Pagan tenant will somehow be discriminated against by a non-Pagan or intolerant landlord. This chapter will deal exclusively with renters because this seems to be the most common form of discrimination feared by Pagans, and when dealing with property, it is the form of discrimination that leaves Pagans the most vulnerable. After all, who wants to be out on the street with their families, their furniture, and their pets?

I have heard a number of complaints over the years: *"The landlord would not rent to us because we are Wiccans." "The landlord evicted us because we are Pagans." "The landlord won't let us have an altar with our gods and goddesses because it is offensive to him." "The landlord won't let our coven meet at our apartment because we are Witches." "We can't have a Goddess-dedicated altar in our home, but the people in the next apartment have a menorah in their window."* The list goes on and on. What can these people do?

In most situations with tenants, landlords have the upper hand. When it comes to discrimination, however, the balance of power shifts to the tenant. Because of strong antidiscrimination laws, a determined tenant or applicant for rental housing who has been wronged can often tie a landlord in legal knots...One of the reasons tenants have more clout in the housing discrimination area is that you don't need to show that the landlord or manager intended to discriminate. As long as the landlord's conduct has a discriminatory effect or impact on members of a legally protected group...you may successfully win a discrimination case....

(Portman and Stewart, *Every Tenant's Legal Guide*, 5/2)

GENERALLY, HOUSING DISCRIMINATION BASED ON RELIGION VIOLATES BOTH FEDERAL AND STATE LAW

As in the area of religion-based employment discrimination, there are some solid federal laws[1] and state laws that protect you from these sorts of practices. To learn more about them, all you have to do is go online and peruse the Website for the applicable federal agency, which is the U.S. Department of Housing and Urban Development (HUD) at *www.hud.gov.* This site provides links to the complete Fair Housing Act (about 31 pages). It also has a very good pamphlet on fair housing, which can be downloaded. Just follow the links on the Website, or go to *www.hud.gov/offices/fheo/FHLaws/FairHousing.Jan2002.pdf.* The pamphlet provides a summary of rights under the federal fair housing law. It also gives the various locations of HUD offices and how to contact them.

Look at the Website for the state agency. Run a check with your search engine or browser for the agency in your state that handles fair housing. You will probably find their Website. These sites carry a tremendous amount of information. There will be a corresponding state agency because most, if not all, the states have corresponding state laws prohibiting discrimination in housing. Check the statutes in your state

In addition, there are some very good commercial Websites that outline the law in this area and provide other valuable resources, such as books on such specific topics as renters' rights, landlord rights, choosing an excellent tenant, reviewing a lease, etc. An example of a good commercial Website is nolo.com, which has several pages devoted to housing issues, landlord/tenant issues, and property purchase issues. Additionally, please see The Cornell Law School Legal Information Institution Website *(www.law.cornell.edu/topics/landlord_tenant.html),* which provides valuable information on the landlord/tenant relationship.

Books are available at commercial booksellers that address these same issues. For example, please see *Reader's Digest: Know Your Rights and How to Make Them Work for You.* This very informative and highly readable book covers myriad of issues, including buying and selling a home, renting property, etc. Another recommendation is *Every Tenant's Legal Guide,* by Janet Portman and Marcia Stewart.

for the applicable fair housing laws. Depending on the state you live in, your state's anti-discrimination law may be more or less broad than the federal statute.[2]

THE FEDERAL LAW

The federal fair housing law is ambitious. Known collectively as Title VIII, the Fair Housing Act (FHA) can be found at 42 U.S.C.A. Sections 3601, *et seq.* The federal fair housing law is sometimes referred to as Title VIII of the Civil Rights Act of 1968. Section 3601 of the statute provides: "It is the policy of the United States to provide, within constitutional limitations, for fair housing throughout the United States."[3] The comprehensive statutory scheme established by the federal law prohibits discrimination in the housing market based on race, color, religion, and/ or national origin. Its prohibitions are meant for both the public and private sectors.[4] However, for some time, there were cases that held that it was permissible, in some instances, for a landlord to discriminate on the basis of race and religion. These cases are compiled at 14 A.L.R. 2d 153. The theory allowing this discrimination was that the federal law was meant to prevent discrimination arising out of some form of government action; thus, discrimination perpetrated by private landlords did not fall within the purview of the federal statute.

The statute has been described as a constitutional exercise of congressional power under the Thirteenth Amendment[5] to bar discrimination in housing. Courts have also asserted that it is a valid exercise of Congressional power based on interstate commerce.[6] Simply put, the federal Fair Housing Act prohibits discrimination of various types, including religious discrimination.[7] The applicable section that prohibits religious discrimination is 42 U.S.C.A. Section 3604, which states:

> ...it shall be unlawful...(a) to refuse to sell or rent after the making of a bona fide offer, or to refuse to negotiate for the sale or rental of, or otherwise make unavailable or

deny, a dwelling to any person because of...religion...(b) to discriminate against any person in the terms, conditions, or privileges of sale or rental of a dwelling, or in the provision of services or facilities in connection therewith, because of...religion....

42 U.S.C.A. Section 3604 (a), (b)

The HUD pamphlet, which can be found on the Internet at *www.hud.gov/fairhousing*, paraphrases the situation nicely. In the areas of the sale and rental of housing, the pamphlet sets forth the types of practices that are prohibited discriminatory practices based on religion under the federal statute:

1.) Refusal to rent or sell housing;

2.) Refuse to negotiate for housing;

3.) Make housing unavailable;

4.) Deny a dwelling;

5.) Set different terms, conditions, or privileges for sale or rental of a dwelling;

6.) Provide different housing services or facilities

7.) Falsely deny that housing is available for inspection, sale or rental;

8.) For profit, persuade owners to sell or rent (blockbusting); or

9.) Deny anyone access to or membership in a facility or service (such as multiple listing service) related to the sale or rental of housing).

(U.S. Department of Housing and Urban Development. *Fair Housing: Equal Opportunity for All*, 1)

As you can see, the provisions of the Fair Housing Acts apply to aspects of the landlord-tenant relationship other than the act of renting. There are certain exemptions under the federal statute. Not all properties are covered. The exempt properties include: owner-occupied buildings with four or fewer rental units, single-family housing rented without using discriminatory advertising or without a real estate broker, and certain kinds of housing operated by religious organizations and private clubs that limit occupancy to their own members.[8] The applicable federal laws can be found at 42. U.S.C. Sections 3601–3619, 3631.

However, what most Pagans will be interested to know is that a landlord renting property covered under the statute cannot refuse to rent to you based on your religion, cannot be more restrictive in selecting you as a tenant based on your religion, cannot treat you differently during the course of the rental based on your religion (such as letting other tenants turn in rents late while penalizing you with a fine), cannot provide different services or facilities to you, or end your rental due to your religion.[9]

The great majority of the cases under the FHA deal with racial discrimination.[10] As opposed to our study of religion-based employment discrimination, the depth of case law for religion-based housing discrimination does not appear to exist. In his article, "Making and Meeting the Prima Facie Case Under the Fair Housing Act," Frederic Schwartz states that the analysis employed to determine racial discrimination in housing cases is usually applicable to the impermissible categories.[11] At least one court has asserted that Title VII analysis (employment discrimination analysis) can be used in Title VIII housing cases.[12]

Generally speaking, the Plaintiff in a FHA discrimination claim need not show discriminatory intent, only discriminatory effect.[13] The burden of proof will be on the Plaintiff to show this discriminatory effect. Although a discriminatory effect is usually sufficient, if a Plaintiff can show a discriminatory motive or a discriminatory related motive as a basis for evaluating the potential tenant, then the Plaintiff will have met a substantial portion of his burden of proof. Apparently, the difference among a case of discriminatory effect, intent, or impact may affect Plaintiff's burden of proof.[14] You must look to how the federal courts within your appellate circuit or within your federal trial circuit have analyzed these cases.

Of course, Plaintiff must show membership in a protected class, such as a racial minority. In the case of religion-based discrimination, this would mean showing that the Plaintiff has religious beliefs and/or practices that are not part of the mainstream. Of course, a housing applicant can be rejected for non-discriminatory subjective reasons, such as a disagreeable personality, or for non-discriminatory objective reasons, such as an inability to pay the rent. As we saw in our discussion of child custody and employment discrimination, you do not want to give the landlord adequate reason to either refuse to rent to you in the first place or evict you once you are in there.

There have been some instances of landlords refusing to rent to certain tenants because such rentals would be in violation of the landlord's religious tenets.[15] These situations present clever defenses by landlords. Additionally, the FHA does not appear to protect religious practices that are criminal. For example, persons who practice polygamy as a part of their religion have not been treated favorably under the federal Fair Housing Act.

In the case of *Barlow v. Evans* (993 F. Supp. 1390, [U.S. Dst. Ct. Utah, 1997]), the federal court refused to extend the protection of the Act to polygamists who claimed that a contract to purchase real estate was broken based on religious discrimination. In denying the polygamists the protection of the Act, the court stated:

> ...Congress did not intend for the FHA to require citizen sellers of real estate to deal with lawbreakers, or perceived lawbreakers, even if the lawbreaking activity is based on a genuine religious belief. Common sense and practicality require such a result. Surely in its effort to provide fair housing to all Americans, Congress did not intend to aid and abet criminal behavior. There is nothing in the Act or its history that suggests such a result. Such an interpretation would require sales of houses that sellers know (or strongly suspect) are to be used as drug

houses, brothels, or even altars for human sacrifices, if such criminal practices were engaged in as part of the buyers' religious beliefs.

(*Barlow*, 1393)

WHERE DO YOU FILE WHAT BASED ON THE FEDERAL LAW?

You have a couple of options here. You may file a Complaint with HUD within one year of the alleged discriminatory act.[16] Again, this sounds like a lot of time, but it really is not. You should probably consult with an attorney before taking any action. However, resolution of this matter could take years, as some experts point out, and so this may not be the best route for you depending on what you want to accomplish.[17]

Suppose you do file with HUD. What happens? The HUD process obviously does not end with the filing of the Complaint. The agency pamphlet, which is available online, outlines the entire HUD process. The agency will conduct an investigation in order to determine if your complaint has merit. If the agency decides that it does have merit, they will attempt some form of conciliation or compromise. If the agency decides that your complaint does not have merit, it will be dismissed. If conciliation is not successful, then there will be an administrative hearing before an administrative law judge (ALJ), and if you are successful before the ALJ, you may be awarded such remedies as monetary damages, rental of the unit you were denied, or some other appropriate action. Remedies before the ALJ can include monetary compensation for actual damages, including humiliation, pain, and suffering; injunctive or other equitable relief; penalties; and attorneys' fees and costs.[18] If HUD determines that you have a serious problem requiring immediate assistance, the agency may authorize the United States Attorney General to go to court and obtain temporary or preliminary relief pending the outcome of your complaint with HUD.[19]

You have the option of going directly to federal court to litigate your federal fair housing claim of discrimination under 42 U.S.C.A. Section 3613(a)(1)(A)[20] and Section (a)(2).[21] Under the federal fair housing statutory scheme, you may be awarded punitive damages.[22] Notably, the federal statute does not limit (cap) the amount of punitive damages that you could receive while some state fair housing statutes do. A punitive damage award can be quite substantial. Consult with an attorney before filing any type of action, such as filing before a state agency, that might jeopardize your opportunity for a punitive damage award.[23]

Because of the complexity and interaction of the state and federal laws regarding where to file what and especially *when* to file, consult with an attorney as soon as you have reason to believe that you have been discriminated against based on your religious beliefs and/or practices. You do not want to lose a good case due to a procedural defect, such as failing to meet the applicable Statute of Limitations.

THE STATE LAW

Because state laws and procedures vary from state to state, you should consult with an attorney in your state, and preferably an attorney in the county where you live, who specializes in fair housing matters in order to find out exactly what the law of your state is, where you stand, and what you should do about your situation under your state laws. There may be an exhaustion of administrative remedies component to the procedure in your state. For example, you may be precluded from filing a court action for religious discrimination with respect to your housing situation without first filing an action with your local state agency. You will probably be able to file actions before a state or local fair housing agency or in the state courts. However, it would be wise to consult with an attorney who has expertise in these areas before you do either so that you take action in the appropriate place and within the appropriate time limitation.

Regarding the substance of the law itself, your state law could be more inclusive than the federal law. To illustrate, Attorneys Portman and

Stewart note that in the state of California, owner-occupied buildings with four or fewer rentals are covered under the California fair housing laws whereas these buildings are not covered under the federal fair housing laws.[24] You may check your state's agency Website for either a quick review of your state law or for referral to the state statutes themselves.

Online searches can yield some amazing results. Look at *www.caag.state.ca.us/ publications/civilrights/OICRhandbook/*, a Web pamphlet bearing the seal of the Office of the Attorney General, State of California, entitled *Unlawful Discrimination: Your Rights and Remedies–Civil Rights Handbook*. See also "Housing Discrimination FAQ" at *www.nolo.com/ lawcenter/ency/article.cfm/obj:*

YEAH, BUT WHAT ABOUT MY LEASE?
UM, AM I SUPPOSED TO HAVE A LEASE?

After you have filtered your situation through the federal and state statutory schemes dealing with fair housing to see if any relief is available to you under these statutes, you must then look to your lease agreement if you are renting. Landlord/tenant issues will be governed by your lease, and these matters are covered by the laws of your state. By way of illustration, in the state of Massachusetts, the relationship between that of the landlord and that of the tenant arises from a contract, either express or implied. That contract permits the renter to use and occupy the specified premises for a consideration, usually payment of rent.[25] Not all state laws will be the same, which is why you will need a competent attorney from the area in which you live to review your lease with you. A lease written in a specific state for premises rented in that state will be governed by the laws of that state.[26]

Just as there were tricky issues involving time limitations, exhaustion of administrative remedies, and exclusions that applied in the area of employment discrimination, some of these issues also arise in the area of fair housing. Finally, as in the other areas of law we have already looked at, you will need to look to your own behavior to determine whether you are, genuinely, a victim of religious discrimination or whether you have simply been a bad tenant. A bad tenant does not pay the rent on time; does not maintain the rental property in a clean and tidy manner; is a poor neighbor and thus, the focus of complaints from neighboring tenants; keeps pets when the lease forbids them; parks in places not allotted to them; fails to pay the utility bills (if the utility bills are your responsibility under the lease); tries to sneak more tenants into the property than the lease allows; etc. Being a poor neighbor can take many forms: excessive noise, loud parties late at night, trash piled up in inappropriate places, dogs that are not kept leashed and defecate on the property of others, or a simple lack of common courtesy and manners.

Should you have a written lease? Yes, because this affords you the best protection: "Because a written lease is always enforceable in a court of law, it is to your advantage to sign one in case your landlord transgresses your rights or reneges on his obligations."[27] There are some very good resources for you regarding the contents of the lease; that is, what the lease should contain in order to best protect you. See "What Should Be In A Lease," in *Reader's Digest: Know Your Rights and How to Make Them Work for You*, 73.

As with job discrimination (you don't want to give the boss a bona fide reason to fire you) and child custody (you don't want to give the court or the Division of Social Services a bona fide reason to take your children away), you do not want to give your landlord a bona fide reason to evict you. So, from the very beginning, you need to be conscious of your behavior and do the things that are necessary to first, find an appropriate place to live, and second, keep the landlord happy so that you can continue living in your happy home.

CHAPTER 7

PAGANS AND LAND USE

INTRODUCTION

Religion and property issues do not end with the rent. Pagans can have trouble with their neighbors,[1] with local tax assessors,[2] and with the townships where they live.[3] Owning property or living peacefully in it is no guarantee that the government is going to keep its nose out of your religion. In fact, the louder and more vocal you are, the more likely it is that the local government is going to come snooping around.[4]

Surely, you are thinking, *if I own my land or my home, I can worship as I please. My coven can meet at my house. I can have my Asatrú kindred over. I can read Tarot cards for my friends.*[5] *The membership of the 501(c)(3) organization to which I belong can meet at our High Priest's house, right? I have rights! Right?*

We all have vague recollections of our right to be secure in our houses and of our right to due process where our property is concerned.[6] The Fourth Amendment to the Federal Constitution states:

> The right of the people to be secure in their persons, houses, papers, and effects, against unreasonable searches and seizures, shall not be violated, and no warrants shall issue but upon probable cause, supported by oath or affirmation, and particularly describing the place to be searched, and the person or things to be searched.
>
> U.S. Const. Amend. IV.

Of particular concern is the possibility that the spiritual observances we make in our own homes would come under public scrutiny. We would all like to believe that the ability to worship in our homes is sacrosanct. Should we be concerned? Yes, we should, because personal

"In dealing with matters of privacy and other liberties, this Court has consistently supported the right of our citizens to be secure in the home, without the disruptive arm of the State intruding into their personal affairs...Nothing can be more deeply personal than [Plaintiff's] desire to worship in the manner at issue here. He is at home. He is in prayer. He is with friends. He is entitled to be left alone." (*State v. Cameron*, 498 A.2d 1217, 1228 [N.J. 1985], concurring opinion of Justice Clifford).

spiritual observances in the privacy of a home are *not* immune from such scrutiny. Issues surrounding religion and the use of property owned by members of devout religious groups are nothing new to the courts. Pagans join a long list of other religious peoples in litigating their Free Exercise rights with regard to their spiritual practices at home. At stake here is the right of the people to worship according to the dictates of their conscience in the place most of us would like to feel the most safe: in our homes. This is a classic Free Exercise issue (see Chapter 3 for more about Free Exercise). As in other areas of the law, which we have previously visited in this book, other religious groups have been slogging their way through courts and zoning boards for quite a while now, too.[7] This is a particularly fertile field of scholastic study.[8] However, before we begin peeling back the layers of this particularly thick artichoke, it is necessary to look briefly at the history of the struggle.

FREE EXERCISE AND LAND USE

Pagan woes over the use of Pagan-owned land and homes have had some far-reaching repercussions. However, there are some recent events that specifically shed light on the problems faced regarding the ownership of land and spiritual observance, as the following real life stories indicate.

In the 1963 case *Sherbert v. Verner* (374 U.S. 398 [1963]), the United States Supreme Court created a balancing test in order to determine whether state action was an unconstitutional burden on religious exercise. In this case, a Seventh Day Adventist was fired for refusing to work on Saturday, which, according to her faith, was a day of rest. She applied for state unemployment benefits and was disqualified for refusing to work on Saturday. The Supreme Court found that there was no compelling state interest, which could justify the denial of these benefits for her religious observance. The *Sherbert* case established that state action balanced against the free exercise of religion could survive only if that state action met the strict scrutiny standard of review: The state action must advance a compelling state interest and use the least restrictive means of advancing that interest.

In 1990, the strict scrutiny test fell by the wayside with the Supreme Court decision of *Employment Division v. Smith* (494 U.S. 872 [1990]). In the *Smith* case, the Supreme Court Justices asserted that any valid, neutral law of general applicability did not require justification, even it burdened religious exercise. The *Employment Division* case involved Plaintiffs who took peyote as part of a religious ceremony under the aegis of the Native American Church. Since peyote is a narcotic and illegal under the state's drug laws, they were fired for misconduct. Consequently, they were deemed ineligible for unemployment compensation, and the Supreme Court sustained the denial of these benefits. It would appear this decision "seem[ed] to sweep away the special protection religion had enjoyed."[9]

In the 1993 *Hileah* case we talked about in Chapter 3, the Santerians who wished to perform animal sacrifice in Florida entered the jurisprudential fray with yet another twist: Courts could strike down governmental ordinances that were occasioned by masked, as well as overt, hostility.[10] In this case, the Court scrupulously examined the evidentiary record before it, which included minutes of meetings where townsfolk had made their agenda plain. No Santerians were going to practice animal sacrifice in their town. The Court focused on this and found that the city's ordinance, although neutral on its face and of general applicability, was still unconstitutional due to is "clear discriminatory purpose—to suppress an unpopular religious practice of a certain minority church."[11] The city ordinance appeared to target the ritual killing of animals, but it made exemptions for Kosher slaughter.

In the wake of the *Employment Division* case, Congress enacted the Religious Freedom Restoration Act (RFRA). Essentially, RFRA overturned the *Employment Division* case and reinstated the *Sherbert* test as the standard of review for Free Exercise claims. Simply put, unless the state action complained of an advanced compelling governmental interest and used the least restrictive means available to advance that interest, a substantial burden on religious exercise would not pass muster under the RFRA.[12]

The RFRA was short lived. In 1997, the Supreme Court declared the RFRA to be unconstitutional in the case of *City of Boerne v. Flores* (521 U.S. 507, 117 S. Ct. 2157 [1997]). In the year 2000, Congress passed the Religious Land Use and Institutionalized Persons Act (RLUIPA).[13] The statute provides, in pertinent part:

> No government shall impose or implement a land use regulation in a manner than imposes a substantial burden on the religious exercise of a person, including a religious assembly or institution, unless the government demonstrates that the imposition of the burden...is in the furtherance of a compelling governmental interest...and...is the least restrictive means of furthering that compelling governmental interest.
>
> 42 U.S.C.A. Section 2000cc(a)(1)(A), and (B).[14]

Thus, the RLUIPA sets forth the current constitutional standard of review for Free Exercise cases. When dealing with land use, this would be one of the major considerations for suits involving a Pagan's free exercise of religion at home.[15] Importantly, the RLUIPA defines a "religious exercise" as including "any exercise of religion, whether or not compelled by, or central to, a system of religious belief."[16] In the case *Murphy v. Zoning Commission of the Town of New Milford* (148 F. Supp. 2d 173, 188 [D.C. Conn. 2001]), which was decided under the RLUIPA, the United States District Court of Connecticut asserted that the beliefs at issue must be sincerely held and religious in nature. Thus, the definition of a religious exercise has been expanded in the RLUIPA from its predecessor, the RFRA.[17] Zoning ordinances that prohibit prayer in private homes improperly violate the RLIUPA.[18]

Clearly, Pagans have not been the only folks to meet resistance when trying to pursue simple spiritual observances in the privacy of their own homes. In the case *DiLaura v. Ann Arbor Charter Township* (30 Fed. Appx. 501, 508 [6th Cir. 2002]), the issue at stake was whether a Catholic lay organization operated out of a private home could hold prayer meetings, with as many as 60 participants. In the *Murphy* case, regular Sunday prayer meetings were held at a private residence, the meetings were not open to the public, there were never less than 10–12 people at the meetings, and the couple hosting the meetings were known to have social gatherings at their home that could include 50–60 guests. The couple had six children, and they began hosting the prayer meetings after Mr. Murphy became sick.

OKAY, BUT WHAT IS ZONING AND WHY SHOULD I CARE?

Simply put, zoning represents a means for the government to scrutinize religious activities whether they are in the home or elsewhere. If you are shocked by this, then you are in good company. Take, for example, the case of *State v. Cameron* (498 A.2d 1217 [N.J. 1985]), involving an Episcopal group. A Deacon of the Reformed Episcopal Church offered his modest home as a temporary place of worship for his small congregation, and every week about 25 people showed up for religious fellowship. One evening, a disgruntled neighbor complained that the noise of the weekly service could be heard 80 feet away, and there were some concerns about parking. The whole matter wound up in court.

In the *Cameron* case, the only complaint apparently offered was that singing could be heard 80 feet away and that once, a guest's car was parked in front of the Deacon's house. According to Justice Clifford, the record did not show a parking lot, no sign, no cross, no defacement of the neighborhood, and no amplification. In writing on the issue of whether the Episcopalian Deacon could use his home as a place for his congregation to meet, a New Jersey State Supreme Court Justice offered his amazement that the "might, majesty, dominion, and power of the State of New Jersey" could be utilized "through enforcement of a zoning restriction against churches in a residential zone, in order to stifle...religious activities..."[19] However, this one complaint was enough to bring the Deacon and his congregation under the meticulous gaze of the local government and finally, into court.

For Pagans, the issue of home worship is very real. For example, look to the case of *The Church of the Iron Oak, Inc., v. The City of Palm Bay, Florida*, 868 F. Supp. 1361 (1994). The Wiccan Church of the Iron Oak was maintained at a private, one-acre residence in the city of Palm Bay, Florida. The owners of the residential property were cited for maintaining a church on their property without the required permit. The whole matter wound up in federal court. Even though the Church of the Iron Oak was not successful in its litigation, the federal court did assume, without actually deciding, that Wicca was a religion within the meaning of the applicable federal law, which at the time was the Religious Freedom Restoration Act.

Zoning is the avenue by which a municipality regulates the use or development of land.[20] Generally, zoning refers to the land upon which buildings sit, while building codes refers to the actual buildings themselves. The power of a municipality to enact and enforce zoning regulations/ordinances arises out of its police power.[21] The United States Supreme court recognizes the power of the states to regulate the environment, particularly where schools, churches, hospitals, and such are located.[22] Zoning laws are somewhat modern, the first comprehensive zoning ordinance having been adopted by New York City in 1916.[23] Zoning ordinances are generally enacted "for the purpose of promoting the health, safety, morals or general welfare of the community."[24] Municipalities generally have the right to carry out their policies.[25]

Zoning ordinances must be facially neutral: that is, they cannot discriminate on their face. They cannot have, as their object, the intent to discriminate. In recent cases brought under the RLUIPA, the courts have checked to see if the zoning ordinances involved were facially neutral and whether there was any evidence of animus or bad intent against religion in either the passage or the interpretation of the law.[26] Zoning ordinances that appear to be facially neutral sometimes may be applied in a discriminatory manner or may have a discriminatory effect, such as the animal slaughter regulation in the *Hileah* case. Such covert discrimination will not pass a constitutional challenge.[27]

A particular criticism of local zoning is that it is peculiarly subject to arbitrariness, abuse of discretion, caprice, and unfairness. Some courts take a dim view of this and find that such decisions can give rise to constitutional challenges.[28] The Massachusetts Supreme Court has stated that to challenge a zoning ordinance, the challenger must prove, by a preponderance of evidence, that the zoning regulation in question is arbitrary and unreasonable, or that it is substantially unrelated to the public health, safety, morals, and general welfare.[29] It is easy to understand why zoning regulations can be particularly susceptible to whim and caprice. They are, by their nature, local creatures. They are enacted by local governments and enforced by them. They deal primarily with local issues, although broader concerns may come into focus, such as a legitimate state or federal interest.

When you purchase property or go to live on it or occupy it, you should take it upon yourself to inquire as to the applicable zoning. Find out what it is and what it allows. This is important because, as with most

How do you find out what zoning ordinances/regulations apply to you? This is not as hard as preparing ritual for the Order of the Golden Dawn. Call up your town offices and ask which department or division handles the zoning code. Then, call these folks and ask if you can obtain a copy of the zoning code. Depending on its size, there might be a cost for copying. Go down and pick it up. Tell the nice people there what your address is, and they can probably tell you how your property is zoned; that is, to what use you can put it. If you are buying property with an intent to operate your 501(c)(3) coven/church out of it, this would be a very good idea. You may or may not be able to operate your church from this location. If you are contemplating the purchase of several acres of real estate in the country for the purpose of a Pagan land retreat or sanctuary where you can host Pagan events, operate your 501(c)(3) organization, etc., you may have to call up the county government to get a copy of the applicable code.

laws arising out of the police power of the state, owners are deemed to be on notice of zoning requirements.[30] This means that you are presumed to know the zoning requirements where you live. You cannot claim ignorance of them as a defense should you be found in some violation of them.

If all of this sounds intimidating, I understand. I have been only tangentially involved in some zoning matters pertaining to property up the road from where I live. I procured a copy of the zoning ordinances from the town offices, read it, and wrote a letter to the local zoning board on a hotly contested local issue involving the commercial use of some property in a residential zone. From experience I can tell you this: the best way to get over being intimidated by a process is to go through it, especially if you are not directly involved or do not have a vested interest in it. So, acquire a copy of your town's zoning ordinances. Read them. Familiarize yourself with those that apply to you. Read your local paper and look under the "Legal Notices." You will probably find notices where landowners are applying for variances from local zoning to do something with their property that varies from its zoning, hence, the basis for the term "variance." Go to one of these hearings and see what it is all about. It might seem boring, but you will know where the hearings are held, who sits on the board, and what to expect should you ever find yourself at one of them for real.

How have Pagans fared when trying to worship as they please on their own property?

It is a testament to the success of religious freedom that such sanctuaries as Ozark Avalon and Circle Sanctuary exist and operate to serve the religious and spiritual needs of the growing Pagan population. However, the struggles fought by both Ozark Avalon and Circle Sanctuary have been arduous and costly. Their ministries do not exist without having been hard fought and hard won. Still, in private homes across the country, Pagans meet with great regularity for spiritual fellowship, religious observance, worship, and other activities central to their beliefs. In light of recent cases decided under the RLUIPA, these spiritual observances should be protected, but the fight is not over yet. Let's take a look at some recent Pagan case histories.

THE CASE OF THE MAY KING

A Pagan group in the Ohio township of Sylvania has faced problems in the performance of their annual spring observance. Spirit Weaver's Church is a federal 501(c)(3) not-for-profit organization. As the name states, it is a church, and it is a branch of a much larger Pagan 501(c)(3) not-for-profit organization, the Church of All Worlds (CAW). On May 6, 2001, at the private residence of Spirit Weaver's priest, the group was celebrating spring with a ritual, which was performed in the backyard of the priest's residence. Care had been taken to shield the spiritual observances from the eyes of non-participants: a fence was erected; plants were strategically placed; and a tent was thrown. However, the rites could still be "seen from an angle"[31] as a walkway was apparently and inadvertently left uncovered. The rites involved a May King and a May Queen. The May King was naked. The ritual was described by CAW Vice President Jim Looman as follows: "'It's like a wedding ceremony...He [the May King] is being bound to the tribe and the Earth...It's a small part of a two-day ritual....'"[32]

A neighbor saw the naked May King and called the police. Once the police arrived, they were shown documents verifying that Spirit Weavers had state certification and nonprofit status. Later, the man portraying the May King was charged under ORC. Ann. Sec. 2907.09, which regulates reckless conduct likely to be viewed by and to affront others. The prohibited actions included nudity, sexual conduct, and exposure of one's private parts. Later, the public indecency charge was dropped, and the charges amended to disorderly conduct.[33] However, this was not the end of the matter.

Mr. Koester, at whose home these events occurred, found himself embroiled in a dispute with the local zoning board. He faced allegations regarding his fence and the use of his residence as a place of worship, such as a church, without a Conditional Use Permit. Mr. Koester employed legal counsel. In a letter to the Zoning Board, Mr. Koester astutely noted: "My home is a private residence at which I hosted a religious celebration. This celebration was no different than a backyard wedding, a Bible study group, a Passover Seder, a bris or a Thanksgiving dinner preceded by the appropriate blessings. I am certain that Sylvania Township has not required conditional land use permits from residents engaged in the listed religious celebrations and it is inappropriate, on that basis alone, to require one of me."[34]

The group met again in May 2002, and again, there was an issue. This time, the alleged problem was loud music.[35] It was later discerned that the loud music complained of did not come from activities hosted by Spirit Weavers. Fortunately, the Yule 2003 ritual in the same location went without incident.

What becomes strikingly obvious in the May King matter is that if your neighbors want to make your life difficult, they can do it. Disgruntled neighbors and neighborhood conflicts can substantially disrupt your peaceful enjoyment of your property. For Spirit Weavers, the problem that split open Pandora's box was nudity. Despite precautions taken to prevent neighbors from seeing what was occurring, neighboring folk still found a way to get an eyeful of what was going on. For all the protestations in this country against nudity, it is still of great interest to most people. In the previously mentioned *Cameron* case, Justice Clifford found it "passing strange"[36] that people could possess obscene movies and fornicate in cars but could not have spiritual meetings at home. As to Spirit Weavers, later problems that emerged from the box were zoning ordinance violations and noise.

I suppose the moral of this story is that if you are going to do anything in the nude in a residential area, you had best do it inside with the doors shut and the curtains drawn. Why is this? Towns have ordinances against public indecency, as we have seen in the case of the May King.

Remember: Government has the power to legislate in furtherance of the public morals as part of their police power. Depending on how the statute is worded, being naked in your own backyard could be a problem, especially if it is likely that someone will be able to see you. This means that anything as innocuous as skinny dipping or nude sunbathing could be potentially troublesome. Where ritualistic nudity is concerned, the clash involves your religious freedom and the right of your neighbor to the peaceable enjoyment of his property. However, neighbors who come uninvited onto your property and spy on you are potentially in violation of trespassing laws and "peeping Tom," or voyeur, ordinances. So, you are not without a certain amount of ammunition in these situations, either. Several forms of trespass may be available to you, depending on the laws of your state.

During parties held at my home in St. Louis, Missouri, the police paid me several visits because neighbors had complained of noise. We tried to accommodate everyone by toning the parties down and taking the parties inside after designated hours. This seemed to make everyone happy, but there is no guarantee such simple resolutions will solve your problems if you have neighbors devoutly committed to running your Pagan spiritual group out of the neighborhood.

In light of recent cases decided under the RLUIPA, it would seem that Pagan spiritual events involving large groups of people at a private residence should be protected activities. As in the case of any civil right, however, this premise—as simple as it sounds—may have to undergo various legal challenges to be proven correct.

THE CASE OF THE CHURCH OF THE IRON OAK

Perhaps no case of discrimination against Pagans attempting to practice their beliefs in the safety of a private home has aroused such ire in the Pagan community as that of this Florida church organized around the tenets of Wicca. In the case of *The Church of the Iron Oak, Inc. v. The City of Palm Bay, Florida,* 868 F. Supp. 1361 (1994), the Plaintiffs who held positions of prominence within the organization were holding religious observances at their home, which was a one-acre residence in the city of Palm Bay, Florida. The city served them with two notices of violation of the city zoning code: According to the city, Plaintiffs were operating a church in a residential area without the necessary permit. While the hearing on the second citation was pending, Plaintiffs filed a Motion for Temporary Restraining Order to restrain proceedings on the second citation and to prevent the city from carrying out any further surveillance of the property.

It is important to note that the case appeared before the federal court on a motion for preliminary injunction, and this type of action carried a specific burden of proof. At the heart of the federal trial court's denial of this motion was the fact that it was brought prematurely. The hearing on the second citation had not yet occurred, and the outcome of that proceeding could "have a significant impact on the case at bar." [37] Thus the court decided to wait and see if the city would find a violation of the zoning code. So the court was obliged to abstain on the preliminary injunction until the city acted. Essentially, the Plaintiffs had not exhausted their administrative remedies as to the Zoning Enforcement Board. The court wanted to know whether the city would actually determine that there had been a violation of the zoning code before proceeding at the federal level.

As we have previously seen in the area of religion-based discrimination in employment, exhaustion of administrative remedies is an important doctrine. There may be procedural hoops through which potential Plaintiffs must jump before they can litigate the merits of their cases. Had this matter been heard before the Zoning Enforcement Board to a final conclusion and then raised in the federal district court under the current federal statute, the RLUIPA, the outcome of the matter may have been significantly different.

THE CASE OF THE GAEA RETREAT CENTER

The Gaea Retreat Center is a 168-acre nature sanctuary within an hour's drive of Kansas City, Kansas. Owned by Earth Rising, Inc., which is a tax-exempt not-for-profit organization under the provisions of section 501(c)(3) of the Internal Revenue Code, the use of the land sanctuary came under fire in November, 2001 when the Leavenworth County Planning Commission voted not to renew a special use permit under which the sanctuary was operating.[38] Beginning in the 1940s as a naturist nudist camp, the land was also a Baptist religious retreat at one time. Under the aegis of Earth Rising, the land sanctuary became the home of the Heartland Festival, a Pagan festival sponsored by the Heartland Spiritual Alliance, as well as the home of other events. You can visit the Website for the Gaea Retreat Center at *www.campgaea.org*.

Apparently, neighbors of the retreat center were uncomfortable with what they believed was occurring at the site. In two online articles written for the *Leavenworth Times*, a staff writer noted that locals feared nudism, paganism, witches, sodomy, and pedophilia.[39] Neighbors apparently expressed concern that such things were "contrary to the 'safe, healthy community' in which they wished to raise their famil[ies]."[40]

The Mission Statement of Earth Rising would plainly seem to militate against such concerns:

> The mission of Earth Rising, Inc. is to promote spiritual tolerance, self-empowerment, personal growth and ecological responsibility by providing an open and natural environment. Earth Rising, Inc. encourages the free exchange of ideas, views and experiences, resulting in greater understanding and respect between groups and individuals.

Earth Rising, Inc. supports ecologically sound practices, and it is actively involved in land and wildlife conservation projects in the belief that the earth and all life [sic] are interrelated and interdependent, and that respect for all life is a Universal Mandate.

(Earth Rising's Mission Statement, *www.campgaea.org/index.php?page=newsletter*)

Additionally, some neighbors complained that the mere possibility of seeing naked people impaired their enjoyment of their property.[41] Some of the camp's neighbors petitioned the Leavenworth County Planning Commission to shut the camp down and cited such reasons as traffic. Earth Rising procured legal counsel and filed suit. Eventually, a settlement was negotiated. Some of the terms of the settlement were published in a Camp Gaea press release.[42] However, some of the neighbors were still not happy, and Camp Gaea officials admitted that they did not get everything they wished for either.[43] The retreat center lost its major income-producing event, which was the Midwest Men's Naturist Gathering.

One interesting development can be gleaned from the *Hileah* case and from the Camp Gaea matter: Persons whose statements show blatant religious discrimination at public meetings may be in for a big shock. While it is true that a person is free to stand up and say that the folks down the street are godless devil worshippers or abominations in the sight of the Lord, those same statements may be a double-edged sword in court. In the *Hileah* case, the Supreme Court focused on these sorts of statements and found that the contested ordinance was so deeply based in religious bias as to be an ordinance of masked, but still discernible, discrimination. So, if these statements are recorded and manage to get into evidence, they can be the downfall of the very legal actions taken to rid the neighborhood of the godless heathens.

So, all godless heathens, take heed. It is important that an accurate record be kept of the proceedings in a zoning matter, or in a matter before the Board of Education, or in court. The resulting transcripts, tape, or video could be crucial evidence in a later court proceeding. If you find yourself at one of these, make sure that someone is taking notes in an official capacity so that these notes will later be transcribed into minutes. You may wish to take a videographer and videotape the proceedings. The local press, even if they are hostile to you, will focus upon sensational statements. After all, sensational statements are big news. Thus, press articles can be useful in terms of preserving discriminatory statements made at these public hearings.

What is a Pagan church to do?

My first reaction is that having a strong legal advocate is a good thing. My second is that the horrific propaganda machine of the Spanish Inquisition continues to lumber on, it seems. There is a tendency, in the public mind, to equate Paganism with all sorts of unsavory behavior. I would suggest that unsavory conduct is not scrupulously reserved for members of non-mainstream religions. In light of recent events involving the Catholic Church and the global scandal involving the sexual activities of its priesthood, I must wonder if neighbors would rally against the establishment of a Catholic sanctuary in their midst on assertions of pedophilia or homosexuality.

Pagans must undertake some form of education in their communities so as to dispel the Inquisitorial equation of Pagans with the boogey man and all his immoral practices. Pagans must be willing to not only celebrate their Sabbats, but they must also attend interfaith meetings and disseminate information about modern Paganism that is more current than the Inquisition's leavings. Additionally, the public must see that Pagans are taxpayers, parents, property owners, and voters just like everyone else. We are concerned about the health and well-being of our children and of the communities we live in. We get out and respond to disasters. We staff local soup kitchens, give blood at blood drives, and stock local food pantries. Basically, it is hard to dismiss organizations and their members who are dedicated to public works and who walk this talk.

In St. Louis, Missouri, local Pagan organizations are making a difference in the public landscape. Having emerged from the broom closet, Pagans in the Show Me state have now become quite public, sponsoring a large annual event called The Pagan Picnic. Held in the heart of the city and now spanning two days, the event has been an unqualified success and attracts attendees from all spiritual backgrounds, not just Pagans. Certainly, St. Louisans are discovering that Pagans are just folks, pretty much like everyone else, and certainly nothing to be afraid of.

Allegations that Pagans and Wiccans worship Satan or practice witchcraft—whether true or not—should not bring about the demise of Pagan-based activities. As seen in this volume, Witchcraft has been afforded protection as a religion under the First Amendment, and if the fallen angel who tempts Christ in the desert is the object of worship in some spiritual tradition, then so be it. Being different or unpopular does not remove a religion from the protections afforded by the Constitution, federal law, or state law.

CHAPTER 8

GOD AND GOVERNMENT

INTRODUCTION

Religion and government, or God and government, have been inextricably bound together for centuries. For thousands of years, the history of the government and of the law has also been the history of religion. From Egypt and their god kings, the Pharaohs, to the current English monarch who is the head of the Church of England, religion and government have usually been spoken in the same breath.[1] The extent of this entanglement was so enormous that it motivated the early Americans in the formation of American government. The separation of church and state that we Americans so blithely enjoy sprang from a history fraught with bloody conflict, and our courts have detailed it extensively in some cases. For example, see the case of *Zummo v. Zummo* (574 A.2d 1130, 1133-1135 [1990]).

In writing about the Virginia Act for Religious Freedom, Thomas Jefferson wrote that the Act's preamble did not include a reference to Jesus Christ so that everyone would understand that the protections of the Act were meant for "the Jew and the Gentile, the Christian and Mohammedan, the Hindoo and Infidel of every denomination."[2] In 1848, the Pennsylvania Supreme Court stated: "The constitution of this state secures freedom of conscience and equality of religious right. No man, living under the protection of our institutions, can be coerced to profess any form of religious belief, or to practise any peculiar mode of worship, in preference to another. In this respect, the Christian, the Jew, the Mohammedan, and the Pagan, are alike entitled to protection."[3]

In order to appreciate the enormity of the great American experiment in separating church and state, we must look briefly backward at this veritable Gordian knot that has so confounded humanity from antiquity to the present day.

In Ancient Times, Rulers and Gods Were Inseparable

Ancient Egyptian civilization spanned more than 3,000 years, dating from 3150 B.C. and the pre-dynastic age. To the Egyptians, their Pharaoh was not merely a secular ruler; he was also a deity. The rulers of the Egyptians "were god-kings on earth who became gods in their own right at their death."[4]

In other ancient civilizations, the king was often closely associated with divinity. Among the ancient Israelites, their god chose kings whom the prophets anointed. When Jehovah ceased to be pleased with his chosen kings, he found others from among the people.[5] Thus the king was not only the secular ruler; he was also the Lord's chosen and ruled in the

Lord's name. There was no separating God and religion from any level of life for the ancient Hebrews, and especially no separation of religion and government.[6] In the Greek city states, the official state religion was that of the Olympian gods. There were state cults and state festivals of religion.[7]

The status of religion during the Roman Republic was that of an official state religion (the Olympian gods and goddesses) with smaller cults in operation. There was religious diversity in Rome: Local gods were admitted into the official pantheon.[8] However, during the age of the Roman emperors, the primary god of the state was Jupiter, with whom the emperor was closely associated, just at the Egyptian Pharaoh had been closely associated with Horus. Additionally, there was an "official cult of Rome and the emperor…"[9] The emperors became gods. Shrines and statues were built to honor them, and the people were expected to worship them and make sacrifice to them. Roman subjects were required to make at least a public showing of the emperor's status as a deity.[10] The Jews resisted this and after the death of Christ, the Christians refused to do it.[11] This refusal to worship at Roman shrines and to make sacrifices to the emperor "seemed in pagan eyes an indication of treasonable intention against the state."[12] Christianity was illegal in Rome during its early days, and people could be prosecuted for membership.[13]

The eventual persecution of the Christians during the Roman Empire is well known. However, after the Roman Empire was split into the eastern empire and the western empire, an extraordinary man came to power. Claiming to have a Christian-inspired vision before a crucial battle, the Emperor Constantine won a significant military victory at the Milvian Bridge.[14] Thereafter, he tolerated both Christianity and the old Pagan religions in his empire. He built both churches and pagan temples. He continued to be the head of the pagan state cult. Although he did not make Christianity the official state religion, he did decriminalize it.[15]

Constantine was also instrumental in establishing Church doctrine. He convened such Christian assemblies as the Council of Arles in A.D. 314 and the Council of Nicaea in A.D. 325.[16] One author notes that in so doing, Constantine had "established not only a great confederacy of both the eastern and western churches but also his own moral supremacy over it, binding Church and State together with bonds that were to remain unbroken for a thousand years."[17]

Although the Byzantine emperor Julian the Apostate tried to bring back Paganism, this effort failed.[18] Finally, emperor Theodosius I, also known as Theodosius the Great, made the old Pagan worship criminal in A.D. 392[19] Christianity was now the official religion of the empire.[20]

The Church and Secular Rulers
vie for control

Byzantine emperors Justinian and Theodosius enacted legal codes that made crimes committed against both God and the emperor heretical in nature, and both crimes were punishable by death.[21] By A.D. 430, heresy had become a civil crime that carried the death penalty.[22] In the West, the popes asserted that the Church was independent from all secular control.[23] By the Dark Ages, the Church had become a major power player: one estimation places Church-held lands between one quarter to one-third of western Europe.[24]

By the time Charles the Great (Charlemagne) was established as the Emperor of the Holy Roman Empire in A.D. 800, both Christian theology and law condemned Pagan forms of "belief, worship, and practice as demonic."[25] The belief at the time was that Pagan custom included human sacrifice to the Devil and offering sacrifices to demons. Charlemagne ordered death for anyone practicing such rites.[26] Church proclamations gave secular rulers considerable power to deal with sorcerers, and in southern England, rulers such as Alfred the Great and Ethelstan threatened death penalties to the wiccan and for wiccecraft.[27]

During the Middle Ages, Pope Boniface VII forbade the clergy pay taxes to secular rulers, forbade the trial of clerics by secular courts, and issued a papal bull in 1302 declaring that every man must submit to the bishop of Rome for the sake of eternal salvation.[28] However, English rulers such as William the Conqueror refused to take a second seat to the Pope. William attributed his victories not only to God, but to his sword.[29]

Other English kings such as Henry II and his son King John had their issues with the Church as well. Henry II ordered the murder of his one-time friend Thomas Beckett, the Archbishop of Canterbury, and King John refused to make certain payments to the Pope, for which he was excommunicated. Later, King Edward III declined to pay any more rent to the Pope.[30]

Church courts were extensively involved in such seemingly secular matters as cases of marriage, dowries, adultery, wills, legitimacy, and contracts. Church courts also presided over matters concerning heresy or church doctrine.[31] By the end of the 11th century, Pope Urban II decreed that all heretics were to be tortured and killed.[32] Popes were commanding crusades and the extermination of whole peoples. For example, Pope Innocent II ordered the murder of the Christian Cathars or Albigensians.[33] Pope Urban II preached the First Crusade between 1095–1099.

In 1229, Pope Gregory IX ordered heretics to be placed in the hands of secular government for punishment: They were to be burned alive.[34] In 1232, he established the Inquisition. In legal cases involving issues of faith, torture was an accepted and common practice.[35] In 1257, torture received official sanction. By the time it was abolished by Pope Pius VII in 1816, it had been a valid legal recourse for the Church for five and a half centuries.[36] Under the aegis of Pope Innocent VIII and his papal bull Summis Desiderantes Affectibus, Heinrich Kramer and James Sprenger wrote The Malleus Maleficarum: The Hammer of the Witches.[37] Literally, it was a manual for discovering, prosecuting and sentencing witches, together with the lurid justifications for doing so. The Inquisition was not just for witches; it was for everyone, including Jews, the native aboriginal peoples of Mexico, of South America, and of India.[38]

The Inquisition never became firmly established in England. Starting from approximately A.D. 668, English witches were tried under a variety of secular and ecclesiastical laws, but they were punished by the state.[39] However, it was a good thing that Bloody Mary, the daughter of Henry VIII and his Catholic Spanish wife Katharine of Aragon, died when she did: Queen Mary may have brought the Inquisition to England.[40]

Finally, the English King Henry VIII, broke from the Catholic church when Pope Clement VII refused to annul Henry's marriage to his first wife, Katharine of Aragon, daughter of Queen Isabella of Castille.[41] In the wake of Katherine's failure to bear him a son, Henry sought to put his first wife aside in favor of an English noblewoman, Anne Boleyn. Enraged by the refusal of the Church to annul his marriage to Katharine, Henry established himself as the "'sole protector and supreme head'" of the Church of England.[42] All his subjects had to disavow the Catholic Church and swear fealty to Henry as both king and head of the Church of England. Henry was both king and Pope in England.[43] Those who would not acknowledge Henry as such were executed, and he pillaged the Catholic monasteries for money. Ultimately, Anne Boleyn fared no better in providing Henry with a son. Accused of adultery and other offenses, Anne was beheaded.[44]

The Tudor monarchs from Henry to Elizabeth I involved themselves in legislation addressing witches and the practice of witchcraft. Under some of these acts, punishment ranged from death to the forfeiture of land and of chattel. Henry and his son Edward were responsible for creating the prayer books used by the Church of England.[45] It was Elizabeth's heir, King James, the devoutly Calvinist son of Catholic Mary Stuart, Queen of Scots, who was responsible for the King James version of the Bible.

COLONIZATION OF NORTH AMERICA

Anyone who thinks that the initial colonization of America was about giving all religious minorities the freedom to worship as they please needs to get a real history book and read it. Perhaps one of the greatest wrongs we do ourselves is to distort our history until we believe the kindergarten pageant version; then, we teach it to our children in this way. We should all try watching the History channel.

The early settlements in Virginia were really the response of Queen Elizabeth I to Spanish expansionism.[46] Elizabeth I attempted to place a colony in Virginia with Sir Walter Raleigh in charge; however, these attempts were ill-fated.[47] James I of England was responsible for the colony at Jamestown, and the expedition that included John Smith in 1606 was motivated primarily by gold lust.[48] When the Jamestown settlers began growing tobacco, they utilized indentured servants and Negro slaves as sources of labor.[49] Defectors from the colony and persons who stole from the common stores were tortured and put to death in heinous ways.[50] Obviously, these endeavors were not about the freedom to worship according to one's conscience.

The Puritan Separatists whom we mythically refer to as the Pilgrims and who ultimately settled in Plymouth, Massachusetts, had denied the supremacy of the king in the Church of England.[51] Fleeing first to Amsterdam but finding its cosmopolitan commercialism abhorrent to their strict religious views, they then went to Leiden: however, the religious tolerance in that community was threatening to them.[52] Arthur Quinn notes: "The tolerance of divergent religious opinions within Holland meant the toleration not just of Separatists but also those who denied central truths of Christianity."[53] After becoming established in Massachusetts and in the wake of threatened Indian attack, their Governor John Bradford decided to reorganize the colony in a way that would make it free from English investors. Under his plan, the colonists would no longer "all work together for the commonwealth. This was an ancient vanity of Plato and other pagan thinkers, as if they knew better than God."[54]

A rather carefree fellow by the name of Thomas Morton had set up a colony nearby that featured intimate relations with the Native American women. Appalled by this and other suspected Pagan practices, such as dancing around a maypole, Captain John Smith went out on an expedition and captured Mr. Morton. He was sent back to England to be prosecuted.[55]

In the Massachusetts Bay Colonies, established further north along the Massachusetts coast, the Puritan colony was to be a Christian commonwealth.[56] The governor, John Winthrop, and his cronies required male colonists to become accepted members of the Puritan Congregation in order to be considered freemen.[57] After all, the godly must never be outnumbered by the ungodly.[58] Regarding the migration of the Puritans to Massachusetts, it has been noted that their fundamental reason for establishing themselves in the New World "was to establish a church-state and not to find religious freedom."[59]

This was not the end of their religious intolerance, however. Roger Williams, a Salem minister who preached the separation of church and state, was ousted from the colony. Thereafter, Williams went into the Rhode Island territory and founded Providence "as a place of perfect religious toleration."[60] Anne Hutchinson, a woman preaching an early type of transcendentalism, had the nerve to declare that she heard God speaking directly to her soul. Exiled from the Massachusetts Bay Colony, she later died during an Indian attack in New York.[61]

However, there were places where religious toleration of a sort did exist. For example, Maryland was founded under the aegis of the second Baron Baltimore, Cecilius Calvert. The landed gentry were English Catholics, while the common people were Protestant. In 1648, the new governor of Maryland made a promise to Lord Baltimore not to disturb the Christians and in particular, not to disturb the Roman Catholics in the exercise of their religion.[62] William Penn, the founder of the city of Philadelphia, was a Quaker who believed that everyone should be free to worship God as they wished.[63]

Given the dark and barbaric miasma of our past, the enormity of the American experiment in separating religion and government represents a landmark event in human history. The first Ten Amendments to the Federal Constitution, known as the Bill of Rights, were nothing short of miraculous and remain so to this day. The United States Supreme Court has commented:

> The Fathers of the Constitution were not unaware of the varied and extreme views of religious sects, of the violence of disagreement among them, and of the lack of any one religious creed on which all men would agree. They fashioned a charter of government which envisaged the widest possible toleration of conflicting views. Man's relation to his God was made no concern of the state. He was granted the right to worship as he pleased and to answer to no man for the verity of his religious views.
>
> (*United States v. Ballard,* 322 U.S. 78, 87 [1944])

STILL, SOME PEOPLE JUST DON'T GET IT

You would think that by now, everyone understands that God and government are like oil and water. They don't mix. However, we are still facing these issues. As recently as June, 2000, Republican presidential candidate George W. Bush, in his capacity as Governor of Texas, signed a proclamation declaring June 10, 2000, to be Jesus Day and therein urged all Texans to "follow Christ's example by performing good works in their communities and neighborhoods."[64] In 1999, John Ashcroft (now the Attorney General) made the comment that "America has no king but Jesus."[65]

Some public school officials insist on displaying the Ten Commandments at public schools despite United States Supreme Court decisions, which hold that this is unconstitutional. In the North Carolina Student Citizen Act of 2001, the North Carolina legislature ordered that the Ten Commandments be posted in public school classrooms.[66] Given the United States Supreme Court decision of *Graham v. Stone* (449 U.S. 39 [1980]), which struck down a Kentucky law mandating the posting of the Ten Commandments in classrooms, one has to wonder why public officials don't spend their time doing other more productive things. It is apparent that people will continue to try and circumvent U.S. Supreme Court decisions, and lawsuits must continually be threatened or filed, as if the courts do not have other things to do with their time. However, in May, 2001, the U.S. Supreme Court refused to hear a Ten Commandment case arising out of Elkhart, Indiana, where a granite marker bearing the Ten Commandments was on display in front of a city building.[67] Some judges also insist on displaying the Ten Commandments in their courthouses, and as recently as November, 2002, Judge Roy Moore, chief justice of the Alabama State Supreme Court, received an unfavorable ruling from the federal district court regarding his placement of a religious monument in the Alabama state courthouse.[68]

On the ABC morning program, *Good Morning, America* that aired on Thursday, June 24, 1999, then Texas Governor George W. Bush made the comment: "I don't think that witchcraft is a religion."[69] Comments like these from top-ranking officials in American government have been found in the mouths of such worshipped icons as Franklin Delano Roosevelt. For example, Henry Morganthau, the Jewish Secretary of the Treasury under Franklin Delano Roosevelt, recorded in his diary under an entry of January 22, 1942, that in a conversation among himself, FDR, and Leo Crowley (who was a Catholic and at the time, the wartime Alien Property Custodian), President Roosevelt said to Leo Crowley: "Leo, you know this is a Protestant country, and the Catholics and the Jews are here on sufferance. It is up to both of you to go along with anything that I want at this time."[70]

Even though the Supreme Court has described America as possessing a wealth of spiritual pluralism, there are still places in America that do not celebrate spiritual pluralism. In such places, people still call Wicca "Devil worship" and harass Wiccans. For example, CBS.com carried a story in August, 2000 regarding Pell City, Alabama. When a county probate judge legally made a Wiccan High Priest's rented home a place of worship, outraged neighbors gathered with placards and petitions, expressing a loud desire to oust the Wiccans from the neighborhood. Police were in attendance.[71]

The Lutheran Synod does not appear to be particularly fond of alternative spiritual traditions, either. On September 23, 2001, a Lutheran pastor participated in an interfaith prayer service in New York's Yankee Stadium. The prayer service, hosted by Oprah Winfrey, included Jews, Sikhs, and Hindus. Saying that the Lutheran pastor in question had joined with "pagan clerics" in the service, the national second vice president of the Missouri Synod of the Lutheran Church stated: "To participate with pagans in an interfaith service and, additionally, to give the impression that there might be more than one God, is an extremely serious offense against the God of the Bible."[72]

One has to wonder if these people went to school in America. The judiciary asserts the following: "'tolerance of divergent political and religious views while taking into account the sensitivities of others' is among the values public education seeks to instill in its students."[73] Pagan school children and their parents no longer seem to be content with religious intolerance. Well they should not be. Most Pagans are aware that Tempest Smith, a 12-year-old girl and student at Lincoln Park Middle School in Detroit, Michigan, committed suicide, allegedly as the result of teasing and taunting from classmates regarding her being Wiccan.[74] In Union County, Tennessee, a Pagan student claims that she has been harassed at school for being Pagan from the time was in the fourth grade until the age of 14. Finally, the parents procured an attorney and filed suit in federal court.[75] Favorable legal precedent involving Pagans exists in this area. Pagan school children have been successful in bringing suit against their school districts. For example, a Michigan high school senior was represented by the ACLU when she sued for the right to wear her pentacle at school. The case was resolved through a pre-trial settlement favorable to the student.[76]

CONCLUSION

By now, the problems posed by a theocratic, as opposed to democratic, government should be apparent. Obviously, our Founding Fathers meant to endow us with religious freedom. Their wisdom becomes more evident in an increasingly agitated world where politically powerful religious factions still oppress perceived "devils," "infidels," or "heretics." Mingling God and government is a bad idea. As a nation, we should be opposed to the theory and practice of spirituality that is forced upon the citizenry, either by the government or by other citizens. Indentured servitude, whether job-related or spiritually based, should not see a resurgence in modern American culture.

CHAPTER NOTES

Chapter 1: Pagans and Their Lawyers

1. A synopsis of this case was published in *Green Egg*. Eilers, Dana D. "The Crystal Seifferly Case: Anatomy of a Law Suit." *Green Egg*, vol. 129 (July/August, 1999): 20–22.

2. The homepage for Ozark Avalon is *www.ozarkavalon.org/*. The history of the tax case can be found in a press release prepared for Ozark Avalon by Elizabeth Barrette at *www.ozarkavalon.org/ property_tax_press_release.shtml*. The Tax Commission's decision can be found at *www.ozarkavalon.org/property_tax_decision.shtml*. You can also download the decision from the Missouri State Commission's Website at *www.dor.state.mo.us/stc/ ozark_avalon_v_lachner.htm*.

3. See Complaint filed in *Cynthia Simpson v. Chesterfield County Board of Supervisors,* United States District Court for the Eastern District of Virginia, Richmond Division, Docket Number

3:02CV888. "Lawsuit Challenges Discriminatory Prayer Policy of Chesterfield County Board of Supervisors: Rights Groups Say Prayer Policy Excludes Some Faiths, Violates Church-State Separation," INTERNET. *www.au.org/press/pr021206.htm.*

Chapter 2: Pagans and the American Court System

1. See *Missouri Church of Scientology v. State Commission of Missouri,* 439 U.S. 803 (1978).

2. See 28 U.S.C.S. Sec.1332 (2002).

3. See "Court: Citizens Have No Right to Bear Arms." The Associated Press, *The Cape Cod Times* (Dec. 7, 2002). The Second Amendment to the federal Constitution states: "A well regulated Militia, being necessary to the security of a free State, the right of the people to keep and bear Arms, shall not be infringed." U.S. Const. Amend. II.

4. Eades, Ronald W. *Jury Instructions on Damages in Tort Actions.* 3rd ed. (Cumulative Supplement, 1997), 13–1.1.

5. For example, the Supreme Court of the state of Massachusetts has stated that suits for malicious prosecution are not favored and should not be encouraged. *Hubbard v. Beaty & Hyde, Inc.*, 343 Mass. 258, 178 N.E.2d 485 (1961).

Chapter 3: Pagans and the First Amendment

1. *City of Boerne v. Flores*, 521 U.S. 507 (1997).

2. *Cantwell v. Connecticut*, 310 U.S. 296, 303 (1940).

3. *Reynolds*, 164.

4. *Thomas v. Review Board*, 450 U.S. 707, 713 (1981).

5. *Alvarado v. City of San Jose*, 94 F.3rd. 1223, 1227 (9th Cir. 1996). See also *Int'l. Society for Krishna Consciousness, Inc. v. Barber*, 650 F.2d 430, 433-434 (2d Cir. 1981).

6. 42 U.S.C.A. Section 2000cc-5(7)(A).

7. *Murphy v. Zoning Com'n. of Town of New Milford*, 148 F. Supp.2d 173 (D. Conn. 2001).

8. Civil Rights Act 1964, 701 *et. seq.* 717, as amended 42 U.S.C.A. Sec. 2000-16.

9. *Yoder*, 215.

10. Ibid.

11. Ibid.

12. Ibid., 216.

13. *Seeger*, 174.

14. Ibid., 176.

15. Ibid., 165.

16. Ibid., 174.

17. Ibid., 174-175.

18. *Torasco v. Watkins*, 495, at fn.11.

19. *Alvarado v. City of San Jose*, 94 F.3rd. 1223, 1228, at fn. 2 (9th Cir. 1996).

20. *Welsh*, 339

21. Ibid., 340.

22. *Seeger*, 174.

23. *Missouri Church of Scientology*, 842, fn. 5.

24. *Krishna Consciousness*, 440.

25. *Krishna Consciousness*, 440, fn. 14, citing *United States v. Kauten*, 133 F.2d 703 (2d Cir. 1943).

26. *Krishna Consciousness*, 440-443.

27. Ibid., 441.

28. *Hileah*, 535–536.

29. Ibid., 531.

30. Ibid., 525

31. Ibid., 532.

32. *Dettmer,* 799 F.2d 929, 932.

33. *Dettmer,* 617 F. Supp. 592, 594.

34. Ibid.

35. Ibid.

36. Ibid.

37. Ibid., 595-596.

38. *Dettmer,* 799 F.2d 929, 931.

39. Ibid., 932.

40. Ibid.

41. September 4, 2002, telephone conversation of Rev. David Oringderff, Ph.D with Chaplain (COL) Janet Horton, Executive Director, Armed Forces Chaplains Board. From email posted at *OurFreedom@yahoogroups.com* on September 4, 2002.

42. *Dettmer,* 799 F.2d 929, 932.

43. *Dettmer,* 799 F.2d 929, at 932, *citing, Thomas v. Review Board,* 714.

44. *Dettmer,* 799 F. 2d 929, 932 (4th Cir. 1986).

45. Ibid.

46. Ibid.

47. Ibid.

48. Ibid., 932-933.

49. Ibid., 934.

50. Ibid., 933-934.

51. *Umerska,* 863.

52. Guiley, Rosemary Ellen. *The Encyclopedia of Witches and Witchcraft.* 2d ed. (New York: Checkmark Books, 1999), 373.

53. *Ravenwood,* 350.

54. Ibid., 352.

55. *Maberry,* 1224, fn.1.

56. Ibid., 1297.

57. *Van Koten v. Family Health Management, Inc.*, 955 F. Supp. 898, 902 (1997), *aff'd*, 134 F.3rd 375 (7th Cir. 1998).

58. *Hurston v. Henderson*, 2001 WL 65204 (EEOC).

59. *Fleischfresser*, 683, 688.

60. Ibid., 687.

61. Ibid., 689.

62. *Rust*, 1297.

63. Higginbotham, Joyce, and River. *Paganism: An Introduction to Earth-Centered Religions*, 120-121. (St. Paul: Llewellyn Publications, 2002).

64. *Doty*, 1084-1087.

65. Ibid., 1082-1083.

66. Ibid., 1084.

67. *Hundley*, 854, fn. 4.

68. *Phillips*, 347.

69. Ibid.

70. Ibid., 349.

71. Ibid.

72. Ibid., 350.

73. Wehmeyer, Peggy, "Witches in Combat Boots: Pagan Rituals on Army Base Cast Controversial Spell," INTERNET. *www.more.abcnews.go.com/onair/closerlook/wnt990623_wehmeyer_story.html*

74. This history was supplied by Dr. David Oringderff.

75. See DODD 1300.17, "Accommodation of Religious Practices Within the Military Services," February 3, 1988 ASD (FM&P), through Ch. 1, October 17, 1988.

76. See *Abington School District v. Schempp*, 374 U.S. 203, 222 (1963); and *Fleischfresser*, 689.

77. *Sherbert,* 402.

78. See French, "From Yoder to Yoda," fn. 6.

79. *Flores,* 536.

80. See Miller, Robin Cheryl, "What Laws are Neutral and of General Applicability Within Meaning of *Employment Div., Dept. of Human Resources of Oregon v. Smith,* 494 U.S. 872, 110 S. Ct. 1595, 108 L. Ed. 2d 876?" 167 A.L.R.Fed. 663 (2001).

81. *Doty,* 1082, fn.1.

82. *Lee,* 591–592.

83. See *Glassroth v. Moore,* Civil Action No. 01-T-1268-N, District Court of the United States for the Middle District of Alabama, Northern Division (2002) at 229 F. Supp. 2d 1290 (D.C. Ala. 2002); and Gettleman, Jeffrey, "Judge's Biblical Monument is Ruled Unconstitutional," *The New York Times,* November 19, 2002. INTERNET. *www.nytimes.com/2002/11/19/national/19COMM.html.*

84. "Lawsuit Challenges Discriminatory Prayer Policy of Chesterfield County Board of Supervisors: Rights Groups Say Prayer Policy Excludes Some Faiths, Violates Church-State Separation." INTERNET. *www.au.org/press/pr021206.htm.*

85. *Cantwell,* 295.

86. See, e.g., *Wisconsin v. Yoder,* 406 U.S. 205 (1972); *Ginsberg v. New York,* 390 U.S. 629 (1968); *Pierce v. Society of Sisters,* 268 U.S. 510 (1925); and *Meyer v. Nebraska,* 262 U.S. 390 (1923).

87. See Gilgoff, Dan, "Not just about sex: The Supreme Court agrees to hear a case that could be a major turning point for gay rights," *U.S. News & World Report,* December 16, 2002, 46.

88. *Prince v. Massachusetts,* 321 U.S. 158 (1944), 166.

89. See *Jehovah Witnesses in the State of Washington v. King County Hospital Unit No.*1, 298 F. Supp. 488 (1967), *aff'd. per curiam,* 390 U.S. 598 (1968).

Chapter 4: Pagans and Child Custody

1. See *Sherbert v. Verner,* 374 U.S. 398, 402 (1963); *Pater v. Pater,* 63 Ohio St.3rd 393, 588 N.E.2d 794, 798 (1992); *McLaughlin v. McLaughlin,* 132 A.2d 420, 422 (Conn. Super. 1957); *Muhammad v. Muhammad,* 622 So. 2d 1239, 1243 (Miss. 1993); and *Munoz v. Munoz,* 489 P.2d 1133, 1135 (1971).

2. In order of appearance, the relevant cases to look at for each of these items is as follows: *Meyer v. Nebraska* and *Troxel v. Granville; Wisconsin v. Yoder; Prince v. Massachusetts; Crowley v. Christensen* and *Jacobson v. Commonwealth of Massachusetts.* For a comprehensive collection of cases involving religion, child custody, and visitation, see ANNOTATION: "Religion as Factor in Child Custody and Visitation Cases," 22 A.L.R. 4th 971 (2002).

3. U.S. Const. Amend. XIV.

4. *Felton v. Felton,* 418 N.E.2d 606, 607 (1981).

5. See *Troxel,* where the cases are all set forth.

6. *Yoder,* 230.

7. *Stone v. Stone,* 16 Wash.2d 315, 133 P.2d 526, 529 (1943).

8. *Matter of Marriage of Knighton,* 723 S.W.2d 274, 278 (Tex. App. 1987); *Frantzen v. Frantzen,* 349 S.W.2d 765, 767-768 (Tex. Civ. App. 1961); and *Salvaggio v. Barnett,* 248 S.W.2d 244 (Tex. Civ. App. 1952), *cert. denied,* 344 U.S. 879 (1952).

9. See *Commonwealth ex re. Rainford v. Cirillo,* 296 A.2d 838, 840 (1972); *C.W. v. K.A.W.,* 774 A.2d 745 (Pa. Super. Ct. 2001); *Cushman v. Lane,* 224 Ark. 934, 277 S.W.2d 72, 74 (1955); and *Morris v. Jackson,* 66 Wyo. 369, 212 P. 2d 78, 82 (1949).

10. *Felton,* 606-607.

11. *Waites,* 331, citing Art. I, Sec. 7 Mo. Const.

12. Ibid., 333–334.

13. *Kendall,* 1230.

14. *Yoder,* 230. See also *Zummo v. Zummo,* 574 A.2d 1130, 1138–1139 (1990).

15. For example, see *MacLagan v. Klein*, 123 N.C. App. 557, 473 S.E.2d 778, (1996); *Harris v. Harris;* and *In the Matter of X. Huff,* 140 N.C. App. 288, 536 S.E.2d 838 (2000 N.C.).

16. See *Harris,* at 764. *See also Gluckstern v. Gluckstern,* where evidence demonstrated that the mother gave child medical care when needed even though she was a Christian Scientist.

17. Van Dine, Lynn, "Mother Wins Custody of Son, Even Though She Practices Animal Sacrifice," *Detroit News,* January 20, 1994. INTERNET. *www.vix.com/pub/men/custody-divorce/cases/ santa-ria.html*

18. See also *Andros v. Andros,* 396 N.E.2d 917 (Minn. App. 1968).

19. See also *Fisher v. Fisher,* 118 Mich. App. 227, 324 N.W.2d 582, 585 (1982).

20. Sec. 210. 165(2) R.S.MO.

21. Massachusetts Department of Social Services. *Child Protective Services: Parent's Guide,* July 2000.

22. See generally *Edwards v. Edwards,* 829 S.W. 2d 91 (Mo. App. 1992); and *Murray v. Murray,* 220 So. 2d 790 (La. App. Ct. 1969).

Chapter 5: Pagans and Employment Discrimination

1. See Eilers, Dana D. *The Practical Pagan* (New Jersey: Career Press/ New Page Books, 2002), 211–213.

2. *Meritor Savings Bank, FSB v. Vinson, et al.,* 477 U.S. 57, 66 (1986). See also *Kishaba v. Hilton Hotels Corp.,* 737 F. Supp. 549, 555 (D. Haw. 1990), aff'd., 936 F.2d 578 (9th Cir. 1991).

3. *Young v. Southwestern Savings and Loan Ass'n.,* 509 F. 2d 140, 141 (5th Cir. 1975).

4. See generally *Hurston v. Henderson,* 2001 WL 65202 (E.E.O.C.), involving Wiccan postal worker Robert Hurston; *Dodge v. Salvation Army,* 1989 WL 3857 (S.D. Miss.), 48 Empl.Prac. Dec. P38, 619 (1989), involving Salvation Army worker Jamie Dodge

who was, at some point, a practicing Wiccan; and *Van Koten v. Family Health Management, Inc.,* 955 F. Supp. 898 (1997), aff'd., 134 F.3rd 375 (7th Cir. 1998), involving a Wiccan chiropractor.

5. Geller, Adam, "Religion increasing source of workplace tension," *The Cape Cod Times,* January 18, 2002, B6.

6. Ibid.

7. *Lynch,* 239, 244.

8. See also *Sarin,* generally; and Geller, "Religion increasing source of workplace tension," B6.

9. All direct quotes from *Turner,* 1027.

10. *Young,* 141–142.

11. Ibid., 144.

12. All quotes from *Weiss,* 1053.

13. Ibid., 1056.

14. Ibid., 1057.

15. *Van Koten,* 902.

16. 29 U.S.C.A. Section 791, *et seq.*

17. *Hurston,* 2.

18. Ibid., 4.

Chapter 6: Pagans and the Rent

1. The federal Fair Housing Act and Fair Housing Amendments Act are codified at 42 U.S.C. Sections 3601–3619, 3631.

2. See generally Portman and Stewart, *Every Tenant's Legal Guide.* 2d ed. (Nolo.com: 2001), 5/3–5/4.

3. 42 U.S.C.A. Section 3601 (2002).

4. *United States v. Henshaw Bros., Inc.* 401 F. Supp. 399 (E.D. Va. 1974).

5. The Thirteenth Amendment barred slavery.

6. See generally *Oxford House-C v. City of St. Louis*, 77 F. 3rd 249 (8th Cir. 1996).

7. Portman and Stewart, *Every Tenant's Legal Guide*, 5/3–5/6.

8. Ibid., 5/4.

9. Ibid., 5/3.

10. Schwartz, Frederic S., "Making and Meeting the Prima Facie Case Under the Fair Housing Act," 20 Akron L. Rev. 291, 292 (1986), fn. 3.

11. Ibid.

12. *Gamble v. City of Escondido*, 104 F. 3rd. 300, 304–305 (9th Cir. 1997). The Ninth Circuit went on to say that a FHA discrimination claim can be premised on either disparate treatment or disparate impact.

13. See *Davis v. N.Y. City Housing Authority*, 278 F. 3rd 64 (2nd Cir. 2002).

14. Schwartz, "Making and Meeting the Prima Facie Case Under the Fair Housing Act," 295-297.

15. See generally Geoly, James C., and Gustafson, Kevin R., "A Fair Housing Enforcement Symposium: A Focus on Special Issues Affecting the Disabled, Families with Children and the First Amendment: Article: Religious Liberty and Fair Housing: Must a Landlord Rent Against His Conscience?" 29 J. Marshall L. Rev. 455 (1996); "A Legitimate Limitation of a Landlord's Rights—A New Dawn for Unmarried Cohabitants," 68 Temp. L. Rev. 811 (1995); Markey, Maureen E., "The Price of Landlord's 'Free' Exercise of Religion: Tenant's Right to Discrimination-Free Housing and Privacy," 22 Fordham Urb. L.J. 699 (1995); "Alaska Supreme Court Holds that Housing Anti-Discrimination Laws Protecting Unmarried Couples Withstand A Free Exercise Challenge by a Religious Landlord—Swanner v. Anchorage Equal Rights Comm'n, 874 P.2d 274 (Alaska 1994)", 106 Harv. L. Rev. 763 (1995); and Johnson, Scott A., "The Conflict Between Religious Exercise and Efforts to Eradicate Housing Discrimination Against Nontraditional Couples: Should Free

Exercise Protect Landlord Bias?" 53 Wash & Lee L. Rev. 351 (1996).

16. 42 U.S.C.A. Sec. 3610(a)(1)(A)(i). See also *Fair Housing*, 6.

17. Portman and Stewart, *Every Tenant's Legal Guide*, 5/21.

18. Portman and Stewart, *Every Tenant's Legal Guide*, 5/21. See also *Fair Housing*, 12.

19. *Fair Housing*, 11.

20. This section of the federal statute provides that an "aggrieved person may commence a civil action in an appropriate United district court or State court not later than two years after the occurrence or the termination of an alleged discriminatory housing practice, or the breach of a conciliation agreement entered into under this title, whichever occurs last, to obtain appropriate relief with respect to such discriminatory housing practice or breach," 42 U.S.C.A. Sec. 3613(a)(1)(A). See also Portman and Stewart, *Every Tenant's Legal Guide*, 5/21–5/22.

21. This section of the federal statute provides that an "aggrieved person may commence a civil action under this subsection whether or not a complaint has been filed under section 810(a) and without any regard to the status of any such complaint...." 42 U.S.C.A. Section 3613(a)(2). See also Portman and Stewart, *Every Tenant's Legal Guide*, 5/21–5/22; and Fair Housing, 13.

22. 42 U.S.C.A. Section 3613(c)(1), which states: "In a civil action under subsection (a), if the court finds that a discriminatory housing practice has occurred or is about to occur, the court may award to the plaintiff actual and punitive damages and...may grant relief, as the court deems appropriate, any permanent or temporary injunction, temporary restraining order, or other order (including an order enjoining the defendant from engaging in such practice or ordering such affirmative action as may be appropriate."

23. Portman and Stewart, *Every Tenant's Legal Guide*.

24. Ibid., 5/4.

25. *Silver v. Atlantic Union College,* 338 Mass. 212, 154 N.E.2d 360 (1959); and *Miller v. Berk* 328 Mass. 393, 104 N.W.2d 163 (1952)

26. See generally *In re L.R. Hollander Co.*, 301 Mass, 16 N.E.2d 35 (1938). Massachusetts State Supreme Court interpreting a New York lease for New York property, and the court found that New York law would be applied.

27. Cohen, Susan. *Reader's Digest: Know Your Rights and How to Make Them Work for You.* 1995: The Reader's Digest Association, Inc., Pleasantville, N.Y., 73.

Chapter 7: Pagans and Land Use

1. Norwood, Stacey, "Pagans Outrage Pell City Neighbors," INTERNET. *www.wiat.com/now/story/0,1597,225274-373,00.shtml.*

2. See *Ravenwood* and *Ozark Avalon v. Lachner, Missouri Tax Commission*, Appeal Number 00-52500, August 8, 2001.

3. Cornett, Larry, and Giglio, Frank, "A Situation in Cleveland, Ohio," Vol. 139 *Green Egg* 28–39 (July/August, 1999), detailing the troubles of Frank Giglio, an eclectic Pagan herbalist owning property in the Tremont District of Cleveland, Ohio. See also *Church of Lukumi Babalu Aye, Inc. and Ernesto Pichardo v. City of Hileah*, 508 U.S. 520 (1993).

4. This is the general observation of one legal scholar. See Carmella, Angel C., "Liberty and Equality: Paradigms for the Protection of Religious Property Use," 37 J. Church & St. 573, 589 (1995).

5. Tarot card reading, fortune telling, etc., are the subject of a fascinating article which collects and reviews the applicable cases. See Sarno, Gregory G., ANNOTATION: "Regulation of Astrology, Clairvoyancy, Fortunetelling, and the Like," 91 A.L.R. 3rd 766 (2001).

6. This stems from our old friend, the Fourteenth Amendment, which states, in pertinent part: "...nor shall any state deprive any

person of life, liberty, or property without the due process of law...." U.S. Const. Amend. XIV.

7. *See State v. Cameron*, 498 A.2d 1217 (N.J. 1985); and *Grosz v. City of Miami Beach*, 721 F.2d 729 (11th Cir. 1983), *cert. denied*, 469 U.S. 827 (1984). *LeBlanc-Sternberg v. Fletcher*, 67 F. 3rd 412 (2nd Cir. 1995)(hereinafter Fletcher I); *LeBlanc-Sternberg v. Fletcher*, No. 96–6149, 1996 U.S. App. LEXIS 31800, at 6 (2nd Cir. Dec. 6, 1996)(hereinafter Fletcher II); and *LeBlanc-Sternberg v. Fletcher*, 143 F. 3rd 748 (2nd Cir. 1998)(hereinafter Fletcher III). See also Smith, John M., NOTE & COMMENT: "Zoned for Residential Uses—Like Prayer? Home Worship and Municipal Opposition in *LeBlanc-Sternberg v. Fletcher*," 2000 B.Y. U. L. Rev 1153 (2000); and Sokoloff, Brian S., "'Airmont' Case Presents Zoning Issues in the Freedom of Religion Context," 211 N.Y.L.J. 1 (1994).

8. For example, see Ghent, "What Constitutes 'Church,' 'Religious Use,' or the like within Zoning Ordinance," 62 A.L.R. 3rd 197 (1975); and Wehener, Ann, "When a House is not a Home but a Church: A Proposal for Protection of Home Worship from Zoning Ordinances," 22 Ca. U.L. Rev. 491 (1993).

9. Smith, "Zoned for Residential Uses," 1155.

10. *Church of Lukumi Babalu Aye, Inc. and Ernesto Pichardo v. City of Hileah* (508 U.S. 520, 534 [1993])

11. *Hileah*, 536.

12. Smith, *Zoned for Residential Uses*, 1156–1158.

13. The text of the statute can be found at 42 U.S.C.A. Sections 2000cc *et seq.*

14. The section applicable to prisoners is 42 U.S.C.A. Section 2000cc-1(a)(1) and (2) which state, in pertinent part: "No government shall impose a substantial burden on the religious exercise of a person residing in or confined to an institution...even if the burden results from a rule of general applicability, unless the government demonstrates that imposition of the burden on that person...is in furtherance of a compelling governmental interest; and....is the

least restrictive means of furthering that compelling governmental interest."

15. For a review of the RLUIPA and some of the recent cases decided pursuant thereto, please see ANNOTATION: "Validity, Construction, and Operation of Religious Land Use and Institutionalized Persons Act of 2000 (42 U.S.C.A. Sections 2000cc et seq.)," 181 A.L.R. Fed. 247 (2002), by John J. Dvorske, J.D.

16. 42 U.S.C.A. Section 2000cc-5(7)(A).

17. See *Kikumara v. Hurley,* 242 F.3rd. 950, 960-961 (10th Cir. 2001).

18. See *DiLaura v. Ann Arbor Charter Township,* 30 Fed. Appx. 501, 508 (6th Cir. 2002); and *Murphy.*

19. Both quotes from *Cameron,* 1226, the concurring opinion of Justice Clifford.

20. 83 Am. Jur. 2d. Zoning and Planning, Sec.1.

21. *Bicknell Realty Co. V. Board of Appeal of Boston,* 116 N.E. 2d 570 (Mass. 1954).

22. *Lark v. Grendel's Den, Inc.,* 459 U.S. 116 (1982).

23. 83 Am. Jur. 2d. Zoning and Planning, Sec. 1.

24. Ibid.

25. *Beale v. Planning Board of Rockland,* 671 N.E.2d 1233 (Mass. 1996).

26. *DiLaura v. Ann Arbor Charter Township,* 30 Fed. Appx. 501, 508 (6th Cir. 2002).

27. *Hileah,* 534.

28. See *Marks v. City Council of the City of Cheasapeake, Virginia,* 723 F. Supp. 1155, 1160 (E.D. Va. 1988). By contrast, the *Marks* court also notes that some federal courts display a reluctance to interfere with local zoning decisions. *Marks,* 1160.

29. *Johnson v. Town of Edgartown,* 680 N.E. 2d 37, 40 (Mass. 1997).

30. *Beale,* 1238.

31. Williams, Jason, "Naked May King's Spring Rite to Result in Indecency Charge," *The Toledo Blade,* May 19, INTERNET.

www.2001nl3.newsbank.com/nl-search/we/
Archives?p_action=list&p_topdoc=1; archive ID number
0105190109.

32. Looman, Jim as quoted by Jason Williams in "Naked May King's Spring Rite to Result in Indecency Charge."

33. "Court Amends Indecency Charge for 'May King,'" *The Toledo Blade*, June 26, 2001, INTERNET. *www.nl3.newsbank.com/ nl-search/we/Archives?p_action=list&p_topdoc=1; archived as Article ID: 0106260082.*

34. Koester, Ron. 2001. Letter to the Zoning Compliance Officer, Township of Sylvania, May 29, 2001.

35. "Naked Dancing Neighbors?" 13 Action News Online, INTERNET. www.13abc.com/ index.cfm?Article=2502&SecName=28&Level=1&SubID=0&Itm= &SideID=&IsItm=.

36. *Cameron*, 1226–1227.

37. *Iron Oak*, 1363.

38. Richmeier, John, "Planning Commission Votes Against Renewing Permit for Camp Gaea, Cites 'Morals' as Reason," *The Leavenworth Times.*

39. Parrish, Connie, "Officials Defend Nudist Camp's Permit Rejection," *The Leavenworth Times*, January 27, 2002. INTERNET. *www.leavenworthtimes.com/archives/ index.inn?loc=detail&doc=/2002/January/27-591-news5.txt*; and Parrish, Connie, "Camp's Neighbors Uncomfortable with Settlement," *The Leavenworth Times*, April 14, 2002. INTERNET. *www.leavenworthtimes.com/archives/ index.inn?loc=detail&doc=/2002/April/14-674-news2-txt.*

40. Parrish, Connie, "Camp's Neighbors Uncomfortable with Settlement."

41. Parrish, Connie, "Officials Defend Nudist Camp's Permit Rejection."

42. Clarity, "Update: Camp Gaea and County Reach Agreement; Special Use Permit Granted," INTERNET. *www.witchvox.com/ wren/wn_detail.html?id=4133.*

43. Parrish, Connie, "Camp's Neighbors Uncomfortable with Settlement."

Chapter 8: God and Government

1. Weir, Alison. *The Six Wives of Henry VIII.* (New York: Grove Press, 1991), 221.

2. Jefferson, Thomas, Autobiography, in reference to the Virginia Act for Religious Freedom, found at *www.nobeliefs.com/jefferson.htm*, from a list of quotes compiled by Jim Walker.

3. Specht v. Commonwealth, 8 Pa. 312, 322 (1848).

4. Clayton, Peter A. *Chronicles of the Pharaohs.* (London: Thames and Hudson, Ltd., 1994), 6.

5. See 1 Samuel 15:1, and 1 Samuel 16:1.

6. Carroll, James. *Constantine's Sword: The Church and the Jews.* (New York: Houghton Mifflin, 2002), 82.

7. McNeill, William H. *History of Western Civilization: A Handbook.* 6th ed. (Chicago: The University of Chicago Press, 1986), 75, 83.

8. Carroll, *Constantine's Sword,* 80.

9. McNeill, *History of Western Civilization,* 176.

10. Carroll, *Constantine's Sword,* 80.

11. McNeill, *History of Western Civilization,* 179.

12. Ibid.

13. Ibid., 180; and Carroll, Constantine's Sword, 85-86.

14. Norwich, John Julius. *Byzantium: The Early Centuries.* (New York: Alfred A. Knopf, 2001), 38-41.

15. De Rosa, Peter. *Vicars of Christ: The Dark Side of the Papacy.* (London: Transworld Publishers, 1993), 48, and 59; and McNeill, *History of Western Civilization* 185, 191.

16. De Rosa, *Vicars of Christ,* 59.

17. Norwich, *Byzantium,* 56.

18. Ibid., 92-99.

19. Ellerbe, Helen. *The Dark Side of Christian History*. (Orlando: Morningstar and Lark, 1998), 28.

20. McNeill, *History of Western Civilization*, 199.

21. Russell, Jeffrey B. *A History of Witchcraft, Sorcerers, Heretics, and Pagans*. (London: Thames and Hudson, 1995), 69.

22. Guiley, Rosemary Ellen. *The Encyclopedia of Witches and Witchcraft*. 2d ed. (New York: Checkmark Books, 1999), 366.

23. McNeill, *History of Western Civilization*, 213.

24. Ellerbe, *The Dark Side of Christian History*, 41,51.

25. Russell, *A History of Witchcraft*, 52.

26. Ibid., 53.

27. Ibid.

28. McNeill, *History of Western Civilization*, 334.

29. De Rosa, *Vicars of Christ*, 95.

30. Ibid., 95-98.

31. McNeill, *History of Western Civilization*, 300.

32. De Rosa, *Vicars of Christ*, 82.

33. Ibid., 211-215.

34. Ibid., 225-226.

35. Walker, Barbara G. *The Woman's Encyclopedia of Myths and Secrets*. (San Francisco: Harper & Row Publishers, 1983), 1003.

36. Ibid., 444.

37. Bunson, Matthew. *The Pope Encyclopedia*. (New York: Crown Trade Paperbacks, 1995), 183.

38. Ellerbe, *The Dark Side of Christian History*, 84-90

39. Guiley, *The Encyclopedia of Witches and Witchcraft*, 368.

40. Weir, *The Six Wives of Henry VIII*, 568.

41. Ibid., 221.

42. Ibid.

43. Ibid., 222.

44. Ibid., 323-324

45. Guiley, *The Encyclopedia of Witches and Witchcraft,* 368-369; and McNeill, *History of Western Civilization,* 389.

46. Quinn, Arthur. *A New World: An Epic of Colonial America from the Founding of Jamestown to the Fall of Quebec.* (New York: Berkley Books, 1994), 5-13.

47. Ibid., 13-14.

48. Ibid., 17, 19.

49. Ibid.,41-42; and Nevins, Commager, and Morris. *A Pocket History of the United States.* 9th ed. (New York: Pocket Books, 1992), 5-6.

50. Quinn, *A New World,* 31.

51. Nevins, Commager, and Morris, *A Pocket History of the United States,* 6.

52. Quinn, *A New World,* 85-91.

53. Ibid., 90.

54. Ibid., 108.

55. Ibid., 109-110.

56. Ibid., 119-122.

57. Ibid., 126-127.

58. Ibid., 127-128.

59. Nevins, Commager, and Morris, *A Pocket History of the United States,* 20.

60. Ibid., 7.

61. Ibid., 22; and Quinn, *A New World,* 144-145.

62. Nevins, Commager, and Morris, *A Pocket History of the United States,* 7-8; and *City of Boerne v. Flores,* 521 U.S. 507, 117 S. Ct. 2157, 2179 (1997). See also Debusk, Thomas L., "Comment and

Note: RFRA Came, RFRA Went; Where Does That Leave the
First Amendment?: A Case Comment on City of Boerne v.
Flores," 10 Regent U.L. Rev. 223, n. 91 (1998). Mr. Debusk
comments that Maryland enacted the first "free exercise" clause in
1649. Ibid., at n. 91. The New York Constitution of 1777
contained a free exercise clause. Ibid., at n. 92.

63. Quinn, *A New World,* 341.

64. Goodstein, Laurie, "Bush's Jesus Day' is Called First Amendment
Violation," The New York Times, INTERNET. *www/
nytimes.com/library/politics/camp/080600wh-bush-jesus.html.*

65. From a speech given by John Ashcroft at Bob Jones University, in
1999. Harkavy, Ward, "Ashcroft to Christian Crowd: Use
Government to Sell Jesus," *The Village Voice,* INTERNET.
www.villagevoice.com/issues/0115/TheVillageVoiceharkavy.shtml.

66. Mueller, Kara, "The School and the Ten Commandments,"
INTERNET. *www.revkara.com/originalworks/
ten_commandments.html.*

67. Gearan, Anne, "Justices Refuse Case on Government Display of
Ten Commandments," *Nando Times,* INTERNET.
www.nandotimes.com/nation/storhy/16818p-310870c.html.

68. For a complete discussion of this remarkable series of events, you
may read the text of U.S. District Judge Myron Thompson's
decision: *Glassroth v. Moore,* 229 F. Supp. 2d 1290 (D.C. Ala.
2002). See also Gettleman, Jeffrey, "Judge's Biblical Monument is
Ruled Unconstitutional," *The New York Times,* November 19
2002, INTERNET. *www.nytimes.com/2002/11/19/national/
19COMM.html.*

69. The transcript for this segment can be found on the Internet at
*www.sacredwell.org/ResourceArchives/General%20Interest/
wiccans_in_the_army.htm.* The corresponding news story is
"Witches in Combat Boots: Pagan Rituals on Army Base Cast
Controversial Spell," by Peggy Wehmeyer, on the Internet at
*www.more.abcnews.go.com/onair/closerlook/
wnt990623_wehmeyer_story.htm*

70. Michael, Robert, "FDR's Antisemitism," INTERNET. *www.kimel.net/fdr.html*. From Entry 27, January 1942, Henry Morgenthau Diaries, in Morgan, FDR, 553.

71. Norwood, Stacey, "Pagans Outrage Pell City Neighbors," INTERNET. *wysiwg://4http://www.wiat.com/now/story/ 0,1597,225274-373,00.shtml*

72. Reverend Wallace Schulz, as quoted in Cooperman, Alan, "Lutheran Pastor suspended over interfaith meet: Missouri Synod wants apology for meeting with Pagan clerics," *San Francisco Chronicle*, July 5 2002, INTERNET. *www.sfgate.com/dgibin/ article/cqi?file=/c/a/2002/07/06/MN157497.DTL*.

73. *Fleischfresser v. Directors of Sch. Dist.* 200, 15 F.3rd 680 (4th Cir. 1994), citing *Bethel Sch. Dist. No. 403 v. Fraser,* 478 U.S. 675, 681 (1986).

74. See Hunter, George, "Teasing and taunting led girl to end her life: Pressures that prompted mass shootings also spur quiet suicides," *The Detroit News,* March 7 2001, INTERNET. *www.detnews.com/2001/schools/0103/07/a01-196600.htm*. See Smith, Denessa, "The Tempest Smith Foundation," INTERNET. *www.witchvox.com/wren/wn_detail.html?id=*

75. Lawson, Jennifer, "Union schools hit with religion-related lawsuit: Action claims student was beaten, harassed for being different," INTERNET. *www.knoxnews.com/kns/local_news/article/ 0,1406,KNS_347_1744221,00.html*

76. Eilers, Dana D. "The Crystal Seifferly Case: Anatomy of a Law Suit," *Green Egg,* vol. 129 (July/August, 1999): 20-22.

BIBLIOGRAPHY

BOOKS

America. Vol. 2. Edited by Hunter Miller. (Washington: United States Government Printing Office, 1931).

Bernbach, Jeffrey M. Esq. *Job Discrimination II: How to Fight, How to Win!* (New Jersey: Voire Dire Press, 1998).

Bunson, Matthew. *The Pope Encyclopedia*. (New York: Crown Trade Paperbacks,1995).

Burn, A.R. *The Penguin History of Greece*. (London: Penguin Books,1985).

Carroll, James. *Constantine's Sword: The Church and the Jews*. (New York: Houghton Mifflin, 2002).

Clayton, Peter A. *Chronicles of the Pharaohs*. (London: Thames and Hudson, Ltd.,1994).

Clifton, Charles S. "A Quick History of Witchcraft's Revival," in *The Modern Craft Movement, Book One: Witchcraft Today*. (St. Paul: Llewellyn Publications,1996).

Crowley, Vivianne. *Wicca: The Old Religion in the New Millennium*. (San Francisco: Thorsons,1996).

Cullop, Floyd G. *The Constitution of the United States,* rev. ed. (New York: Mentor, 1999).

De Rosa, Peter. *Vicars of Christ: The Dark Side of the Papacy*. (London: Transworld Publishers, 1993).

Dickerson, Darby, and Association of Legal Writing Directors. *ALWD Citation Manual: A Professional System of Citation*. (Gaithersburg: Aspen Law and Business, 2000).

Dollison, John. *Pope-Pourri*. (New York: Simon and Schuster, 1994).

Eades. Ronald W. *Jury Instructions on Damages in Tort Actions*. 3d ed. Cumulative Supplement, 1997).

Eilers, Dana. *The Practical Pagan*. (New Jersey: Career Press/New Page Books, 2002).

Eisler, Riane. *The Chalice and the Blade*. (San Francisco: Harper Collins,1988).

Ellerbe, Helen. *The Dark Side of Christian History*. (Orlando: Morningstar and Lark, 1998).

Ellis, Joseph J. *Founding Brothers*. (New York: First Vintage Books, 2002).

Guiley, Rosemary Ellen. *The Encyclopedia of Witches and Witchcraft*. 2d ed. (New York: Checkmark Books,1999).

Hayes, Michael. *The Egyptians*. (New York: Rizzoli International Publications, Inc., 1998).

Higginbotham, Joyce, and River. *Paganism: An Introduction to Earth-Centered Religions*. (St. Paul: Llewellyn Publications, 2002).

Karst, Patrice. *God Made Easy*. (New York: Warner Books, 1997).

McNeill, William H. *History of Western Civilization: A Handbook.* 6th ed. (Chicago: The University of Chicago Press,1986).

Nevins, Allan, Henry Steele Commager, and Jeffrey Morris. *A Pocket History of the United States.* 9th ed. (New York: Pocket Books,1992).

Norwich, John Julius. *Byzantium: The Early Centuries.* (New York: Alfred A. Knopf 2001).

Hopman, Ellen Evert and Lawrence Bond. *People of the Earth: The New Pagans Speak Out.* (Rochester: Destiny Books, 1996).

Portman, Janet, and Marcia Stewart. *Every Tenant's Legal Guide.* 2d ed. (Nolo.com: 2001).

Quinn, Arthur. *A New World: An Epic of Colonial America from the Founding of Jamestown to the Fall of Quebec.* (New York: Berkley Books,1994).

Reader's Digest: Know Your Rights and How to Make Them Work for You. (Pleasantville: The Reader's Digest Association, Inc.,1995).

Robbins, Rossell Hope. *The Encyclopedia of Witchcraft & Demonology.* (New York: Bonanza Books, 1981).

Russell, Jeffrey B. *A History of Witchcraft, Sorcerers, Heretics, and Pagans.* (London: Thames and Hudson, 1995).

Shaw, Ian and Paul Nicholson, in association with The British Museum. *The Dictionary of Ancient Egypt.* (New York: Harry N. Abrams, Inc.,1995).

Strayer, Joseph R., Hans W. Gatzke, and E. Harris Harbison , *The Mainstream of Civilization Since 1500.* 4th ed. (New York: HBJ College and School Division, 1984).

The Holy Bible, rev. version. (Dallas: The World Publishing Company, The Melton Book Company, 1962).

The Life and Times of Louis XIV. Edited by Enzo Orlandi. (Philadelphia: Curtis Books; and New York: The Curtis Publishing Company,1967).

Treaties and Other International Acts of The United States of America. Edited by Hunter Miller. Vol. 2. (Washington: United States Government Printing Office, 1931).

Walker, Barbara G. *The Woman's Encyclopedia of Myths and Secrets.* (San Francisco: Harper and Row Publishers,1983).

Weir, Alison. *The Six Wives of Henry VIII.* (New York: Grove Press, 1991).

Wenner, Jann. *Twenty Years of Rolling Stone: What a Long, Strange Trip It's Been.* (New York: Straight Arrow Publishers, 1987).

Wilson, Hilary. *People of the Pharaohs: From Peasant to Courtier.* (London: Brockhampton Press,1999).

Zell, Oberon. "The CAW Vision into Tomorrow," in *Church of All Worlds Handbook.* 3d ed. (Autumn 1997).

Case Law

Abington School District v. Schempp, 374 U.S. 203, 222 (1963).

Alaniz v. Alaniz, 867 S.W.2d 54 (Tex. App. 1993).

Alexis v. McDonald's Restaurants of Massachusetts, Inc., 67 F. 3rd 31, on remand, 1996 WL 463675.

Alvarado v. City of San Jose, 94 F. 3rd. 1223 (9th Cir. 1996).

Angel v. Angel, 2 Ohio Op.2d 136, 140 N.E.2d 86 (1956).

Andros v. Andros, 396 N.W.2d 917 (Minn. App. 1986).

Barlow v. Evans, 993 F. Supp. 1390 (U.S. Dst. Ct. Utah, 1997).

Beale v. Planning Board of Rockland, 671 N.E.2d 1233 (Mass. 1996).

Bell v. Wolfish, 441 U.S. 520 (1979).

Bicknell Realty Co. V. Board of Appeal of Boston, 116 N.E. 2d 570 (Mass. 1954).

Blalock v. Metals Trades, Inc., 775 F. 2d 703 (6th Cir. 1985).

Cantwell v. Connecticut, 310 U.S. 296 (1940).

Carter v. Commissioner of Correction, 681 N.E.2d 1255 (Mass. App.1997).

Chatman v. Gentle Dental Center of Waltham, 973 F. Supp. 228 (D. Mass. 1997).

Church of Iron Oak v. Palm Bay, 868 F. Supp. 1361 (M.D. Fla. 1994), aff'd., 110 F.3rd 777, (11th Cir. 1997).

Church of Lukumi Babalu Aye, Inc. and Ernesto Pichardo v. City of Hileah, 508 U.S. 520 (1993).

City of Boerne v. Flores, 521 U.S. 507, 117 S. Ct. 2157 (1997)

Clift v. Clift, 346 So. 2d 429 (Ala. Civ. App. 1977)

Commonwealth v. LePore, 666 N.E. 2d. 152 (Mass. App. 1996).

Commonwealth v. Nesbit, 34 Pa. 398(1859).

Commonwealth ex rel. Rainford v. Cirillo, 296 A.2d 838 (1972).

Crowley v. Christensen, 137 U.S. 86 (1890).

Crystal Seifferly v. Lincoln Park Public Schools, Cause No. 90 DV-60070 DT, U.S. District Court, Eastern District of Michigan, Southern Division.

Cuddyer v. Stop & Shop Supermarket Co., 750 N.E.2d 928 (2001).

Cushman v. Lane, 224 Ark. 934, 277 S.W.2d 72 (1955).

C.W. v. K.A.W., 774 A.2d 745 (Pa. Super. Ct. 2001).

Cynthia Simpson v. Chesterfield County Board of Supervisors, United States District Court for the Eastern District of Virginia, Richmond Division, Docket Number 3:02CV888.

Davis v. Beason, 133 U.S. 333 (1890).

Davis v. N.Y. City Housing Authority, 278 F. 3rd 64 (2nd Cir. 2002).

DeSanctis v. Lynn Water & Sewer Com'n., 666 N.E.2d 1292 (Mass. 1996).

Dettmer v. Landon, 617 F. Supp. 592 (E.D. Va. 1985).

Dettmer v. Landon, 799 F.2d 929 (4th Cir. 1986).

DiLaura v. Ann Arbor Charter Township, 30 Fed. Appx. 501, 508 (6th Cir. 2002).

Doty v. Lewis, 995 F. Supp. 1081 (D. Ariz. 1998).

Dodge v. Salvation Army, 1989 WL 3857 (S.D. Miss.), 48 Empl. Prac. Dec. P38, 619 (1989).

Edwards v. Aguillard, 482 U.S. 578 (1987).

Edwards v. Edwards, 829 S.W. 2d 91 (Mo. App. 1992).

Employment Division v. Smith, 494 U.S. 872 (1990).

Enos v. Brown, 236 N.E.2d 919 (Mass. 1968).

Fant v. New England Power Service, 239 F.3rd 8 (1st Cir. 2001).

Felton v. Felton, 418 N.E. 2d 606 (1981).

Fisher v. Fisher, 118 Mich. App. 227, 324 N.W.2d 582 (1982).

Fleischfresser v. Directors of Sch. Dst. 200, 15 F.3rd 680 (7th Cir. 1994).

Frantzen v. Frantzen, 349 S.W.2d 765 (Tex. Civ. App. 1961).

Gamble v. City of Escondido, 104 F. 3rd 300 (9th Cir. 1997).

Ginsberg v. New York, 390 U.S. 629 (1968).

Glassroth v. Moore, District Court of the U.S. for the Middle District of Alabama, Northern Division, Civil Action No. 01-T-1268-N (Nov. 18, 2002); 229 F. Supp. 2d 1290 (D.C. Ala. 2002).

Gluckstern v. Gluckstern, 158 N.Y.S2d 504, 17 Misc. 83 (1956).

Goldberg v. City of Philadelphia, 65 Emp. Prac. Dec. P43,221. 19994 SL 313030 (E.D. Pa. 1994).

Goodman v. Carter, 2001 WL 1519417 (N.D. Ill.), U.S. Dis. LEXIS 9213 (U.S. District Court for the Northern District of Illinois, Eastern Division).

Good News Club. V. Milford Central School, 533 U.S. 98, 121 S. Ct. 2093 (2001).

Graham v. Stone, 449 U.S. 39 (1980).

Grosz v. City of Miami Beach, 721 F.2d 729 (11th Cir. 1983), cert. denied, 469 U.S. 827 (1984).

Hamel v. Board of Health, 664 N.E.2d 1199, 1200 (Mass. App. 1996).

Harris v. Harris, 343 So.2d 762 (Miss. 1977).

Harris v. Forklift Systems, Inc., 510 U.S. 17, 114 S.Ct. 367 (1993).

Holy Spirit Assn. for Unification of World Christianity v. Tax Commission of City of N. Y., 438 N.Y.S. 2d 521 (App. Div. 1981).

Hubbard v. Beaty & Hyde, Inc., 343 Mass. 258, 178 N.E.2d 485 (1961).

Hurston v. Henderson, 2001 WL 65204 (EEOC).

Int'l. Society for Krishna Consciousness, Inc. v. Barber, et al., 650 F. 2d 430 (2d Cir. 1981).

In re Laura Doyle, 16 Mo. App. 159 (1884).

In re Marriage of Murga, 103 Cal App 3d 498, 163 Cal Rptr. 79 (1980).

In the Matter of X. Huff, 140 N.C. App. 288, 536 S.E.2d 838 (2000 N.C.).

Isbel v. McAbee, 448 So. 2d 372 (Ala. App. 1984).

Jacobs v. Jacobs, 25 Ill. App. 3rd 175, 323 N.E.2d 21 (1974).

Jacobson v. Commonwealth of Massachusetts, 197 U.S. 11 (1905).

Jehovah Witnesses in the State of Washington v. King County Hospital Unit No. 1, 298 F. Supp. 488 (1967), aff'd. per curiam, 390 U.S. 598 (1968).

Kishaba v. Hilton Hotels Corp., 737 F. Supp. 549, 555 (D. Haw.1990), aff'd., 936 F.2d 578 (9th Cir. 1991).

Kendall v. Kendall, 426 Mass. 238, 687 N.E.2d 1228 (1997).

King v. First, 46 Mass. App. Ct. 372, 705 N.E.2d 1172 (1999).

Kirchner v. Caughey, 606 A.2d 257 (1992).

Lamb's Chapel v. Center Moriches Union Free School District, 508 U.S. 384 (1993).

Lark v. Grendel's Den, Inc., 459 U.S. 116 (1982).

LeBlanc-Sternberg v. Fletcher, 67 F. 3rd 412 (2nd Cir. 1995)(hereinafter Fletcher I).

LeBlanc-Sternberg v. Fletcher, No. 96-6149, 1996 U.S. App. LEXIS 31800, (2nd Cir. Dec. 6, 1996)(hereinafter Fletcher II).

LeBlanc-Sternberg v. Fletcher, 143 F. 3rd 748 (2nd Cir. 1998)(hereinafter Fletcher III).

Lee v. Weisman, 505 U.S. 577 (1992).

Lemon v. Kurtzman, 403 U.S. 602 (1971).

Lynch v. Pathmark Supermarkets, 987 F. Supp. 236 (D.C.S.N.Y. 1997).

Maberry v. McKune, 24 F. Supp.2d 1222 (D.Ka. 1998).

MacLagan v. Klein, 123 N.C. App. 557, 473 S.E.2d 778 (1996).

Marks v. City Council of the City of Cheasapeake, Virginia, 723 F. Supp. 1155, 1160 (E.D. Va. 1988).

Mathews v. Ocean Spray Cranberries, Inc., 696 N.E.2d 1303, 426 Mass. 122 (1997).

Matter of Marriage of Knighton, 723 S.W.2d 274, 278 (Tex. App. 1987).

McLaughlin v. McLaughlin, 132 A.2d 420 (Conn. Super. 1957).

Meltebeke v. Bureau of Labor & Industries, 852 P.2d 859 (1993).

Meritor Savings Bank, FSB v. Vinson, et al., 477 U.S. 57 (1986).

Meyer v. Nebraska, 262 U.S. 390 (1923).

Miller v. Berk, 328 Mass. 393, 104 N.E.2d 163 (1952).

Missouri Church of Scientology v. State Commission of Missouri, 560 S.W.2d 837 (Mo. 1977).

Missouri Church of Scientology v. State Tax Commission of Missouri, 439 U.S. 803 (1978).

Mitchell v. Angelone, 82 F. Supp. 2d 485 (Dst. Ct. E. Dst.Va. 1999).

Muhammed v. Muhammed, 622 So.2d 1239 (Miss. 1993).

Murphy v. Zoning Com'n. of Town of New Milford, 148 F. Supp.2d 173 (D. Conn. 2001).

Morris v. Jackson, 66 Wyo. 369, 212 P2d 78 (1949).

Munoz v. Munoz, 489 P.2d 1133 (1971).

Murray v. Murray, 220 So. 2d 790 (1969).

Newdow v. U.S. Congress, et al., 292 F.3rd 597 (9th Cir. 2002).

Nonnenman v. Elshimy, 615 A.2d 799 (1992).

O'Lone v. Estate of Shabazz, 482 U.S. 342 (1987).

Oxford House-C v. City of St. Louis, 77 F. 3rd 249 (8th Cir. 1996).

Ozark Avalon v. Lachner, Missouri State Tax Commission, Appeal Number 00-52500 (August 8, 2001).

Pater v. Pater, 63 Ohio St.3rd 393, 588 N.E.2d 794 (1992).

People v. Umerska, 94 Mich. App. 799, 289 N.W.2d 858 (1980).

Pierce v. Society of Sisters, 268 U.S. 510 (1925).

Prince v. Massachusetts, 321 U.S. 158 (1944).

Quercia v. Allmerica Financial, 84 F. Supp.2d 222 (D.C. Mass. 2000).

Reynolds v. United States, 98 U.S. 145 (1878).

R.A. v. City of St. Paul, Minnesota, 505 U.S. 377 (1992).

R.J.A. v. G.M.A., 969 S.W.2d 241 (Mo. App. 1998).

R.H. v. B.F., 653 N.E.2d 195 (1985), review granted, 655 N.E.2d 1277, aff'd., 664 N.E.2d 434.

Roemer v. Board of Pub. Works, 426 U.S. 736 (1976).

Rouser v. White, 944 F. Supp. 1447 (E.D. Cal. 1996).

Rust v. Clark, 883 F. Supp. 1293 (D. Neb. 1995).

Salvaggio v. Barnett, 248 S.W.2d 244 (Tex. Civ. App. 1952), cert. denied, 344 U.S. 879 (1952).

Sarin v. Raytheon, 905 F. Supp. 49 (D.C. Mass. 1995).

Sherbert v. Verner, 374 U.S. 398 (1963).

Silver v. Atlantic Union College, 338 Mass. 212, 154 N.E.2d 360 (1959).

Smith v. Anchor Building Corp., 536 F. 2d 231 (8th Cir. 1976).

Smith v. Hundley, 190 F. 3rd 852 (8th Cir. 1999).

Specht v. Commonwealth, 8 Pa. 312 (1848).

State v. Cameron, 498 A.2d 1217 (N.J. 1985).

State v. Leitner, 272 Kan. 398, 34 P.3rd 42 (2001).

Stone v. Stone, 16 Wash.2d 315, 133 P.2d 526 (1943).

Thomas v. Review Board, 450 U.S. 707 (1981).

Torasco v. Watkins, 367 U.S. 488 (1961).

Troxel v, Granville, 530 U.S. 57, 120 S. Ct. 2054 (2000).

Turner v. Safley, 482 U.S. 78 (1987).

United States v. Ballard, 322 U.S. 78 (1944).

United States v. Henshaw Bros., Inc. 401 F. Supp. 399 (E.D. Va. 1974).

United States v. Kauten, 133 F.2d 703 (2d Cir. 1943).

United States v. Macintosh, 283 U.S. 605 (1931).

United States v. Phillips, 42 M.J. 346 (1995).

United States v. Seeger, 380 U.S. 163 (1965).

Van Koten v. Family Health Management, Inc., 955 F. Supp. 898 (1997), aff'd, 134 F.3rd 375 (7th Cir. 1998).

Waites v. Waites, 567 S.W. 2d 326 (Mo. 1978).

Wallace v. Jaffree, 472 U.S. 38, 49–50 (1985).

Wallis v. Spencer, 202 F.3rd. 1126 (9th Cir. 2000).

Warrick v. Lane, Texas Court of Appeals, 4th District, San Antonio, No. 16064 (April 11, 1979).

Welsh v. United States, 398 U.S. 333 (1970).

Weiss v. U.S., 595 F. Supp. 1050 (D.C. Va. 1984).

West Virginia v. State Board of Education v. Barnette, 319 U.S. 624 (1943).

Wisconsin v. Yoder, 406 U.S. 205 (1972).

Young v. Southwestern Sav. and Loan Ass'n., 409 F.2d 140 (5th Cir. 1995).

Zorach v. Clauson, 343 U.S. 306 (1952).

Zummo v. Zummo, 394 Pa. Super. 30, 574 A.2d 1130 (1990).

FEDERAL AND STATE CONSTITUTIONS

U.S. Const. Preamble

U.S. Const. Amend I.

U.S. Const. Amend II.

U.S. Const. Amend IV.

U.S. Const. Amend V.

U.S. Const. Amend XIII.

U.S. Const. Amend XIV.

Mo. Const. Art. I, Section 7.

Texas Const. Art. I, Section 6.

FEDERAL AND STATE STATUTES

Universal Military Training and Service Act, Sec. 6J, as amended 50 U.S.C. Ap Sec. 456(j)(1948).

42 U.S.C. Section. 1983.

42 U.S.C.A. Section 2000cc-5(7)(A).

42 U.S.C.A. Section 2000e(j).

42 U.S.C. Sections 3601, 3619, 3631.

42 U.S.C.A. Section 3613(a)(1)(A).

42 U.S.C.A. Section 2000cc1(a)(1), (2).

42 U.S.C.A. Section 3613(a)(2).

29 U.S.C.A. Section 791, *et seq.*

Civil Rights Act 1964, 701, *et seq.* 717, as amended 42 U.S.C.A. Section 2000-16.

M.G.L.A. Chapter 108, Section 31.

M.G.L.A. Ch. 208, Section 31.

M.G.L.A. Ch. 119, Sections 51A, et *seq*, and M.G.L.A. Ch. 72.

M.G.L.A. Ch. 119, Section 51A.

M.G.L.A. Ch. 151(B)(4), *et seq.*

Michigan Stat. Ann. Sec. 25.312 (3).

MO. V.A.M.S. Sec. 425.375(2)(1)-(8).

MO. V.A.M.S. Sec. 210.115(1).

MO. V.A.M.S. Sec. 210.115(4).

MO. V.A.M.S. Sec. 425.375(2)(1)-(8).

Federal and state Rules of Procedure

Massachusetts Rule of Civil Procedure 12(b)(6).

Massachusetts Rule of Civil Procedure 3.

Massachusetts Rule of Civil Procedure 4.

Massachusetts Rule of Civil Procedure 12(a).

Massachusetts Rule of Civil Procedure 55.

Massachusetts Rule of Civil Procedure 60(b).

Massachusetts Rule of Civil Procedure 26, *et seq.*

Massachusetts Rule of Civil Procedure 33.

Massachusetts Rule of Civil Procedure 34.

Massachusetts Rule of Civil Procedure 37.

Massachusetts Rule of Civil Procedure 50, *et seq.*

Journals and periodicals—print

"A Legitimate Limitation of a Landlord's Rights—A New Dawn for Unmarried Cohabitants," 68 Temp. L. Rev. 811 (1995).

"Jury Convicts sect leader: Jacques Robidoux guilty of starving baby to death," *The Cape Cod Times*, June 15 2002, vol. 66, no. 142, page A4.

ANNOTATION: "Religion as a Factor in Child Custody and Visitation Cases," 22 A.L.R. 4th 971 (2202).

ANNOTATION: "Validity, Construction, and Operation of Religious Land Use and Institutionalized Persons Act of 2000 (42 U.S.C.A. Sections 2000cc et seq.)," 181 A.L.R. Fed. 247 (2002), by John J. Dvorske, J.D.

ANNOTATION: "What Constitutes Religious Harassment in Employment in Violation of Title VII of Civil Rights Act of 1964," 149 A.L.R. Fed. 405 (2001), by David J. Stephenson, Jr., J.D., Ph.D.

Carmella, Angel C., "Liberty and Equality: Paradigms for the Protection of Religious Property Use," 37 J. Church & St. 573 (1995), page 589.

"Alaska Supreme Court Holds that Housing Anti-Discrimination Laws Protecting Unmarried Couples Withstand A Free Exercise Challenge by a Religious Landlord—*Swanner v. Anchorage Equal Rights Comm'n*," 874 P.2d 274 (Alaska 1994), 106 Harv. L. Rev. 763 (1995).

Cornett, Larry, and Frank Giglio, "A Situation in Cleveland, Ohio," *Green Egg*, vol. 139 (July/August 1999), pages 28–39.

"Court: Citizens Have No Right to Bear Arms," *The Cape Cod Times*, December 7 2002.

Eilers, Dana D., "The Crystal Seifferly Case: Anatomy of a Law Suit," *Green Egg*, vol. 129 (July/August 1999), pages 20–22.

French, Rebecca, "ARTICLE: From Yoder to Yoda: Models of Traditional, Modern, and Postmodern Religion in U.S. Constitutional Law," 41 ARIZ. L. REV. 49 (1999).

Geller, Adam, "Religion increasing source of workplace tension," *The Cape Cod Times*, January 18 2003, page B6.

Geoly, James C., and Kevin R. Gustafson, "A Fair Housing Enforcement Symposium: A Focus on Special Issues Affecting the Disabled, Families with Children and the First Amendment:

Article: Religious Liberty and Fair Housing: Must a Landlord Rent Against His Conscience?" 29 J. Marshall L. Rev. 455 (1996).

Ghent, "What Constitutes 'Church,' 'Religious Use,' or the like within Zoning Ordinance," 62 A.L.R. 3rd 197 (1975).

Gilgoff, Dan, "Not just about sex: The Supreme Court agrees to hear a case that could be a major turning point for gay rights," *U.S. News & World Report,* December 16 2002.

Johnson, Scott A., "The Conflict Between Religious Exercise and Efforts to Eradicate Housing Discrimination Against Nontraditional Couples: Should Free Exercise Protect Landlord Bias?" 53 Wash & Lee L. Rev. 351 (1996).

Markey, Maureen E., "The Price of Landlord's 'Free' Exercise of Religion: Tenant's Right to Discrimination-Free Housing and Privacy," 22 Fordham Urb. L.J. 699 (1995).

Miller, Robin Cheryl, "What Laws are Neutral and of General Applicability Within Meaning of *Employment Div., Dept. of Human Resources of Oregon v. Smith,* 494 U.S. 872, 110 S. Ct. 1595, 108 L. Ed. 2d 876?" 167 A.L.R.Fed. 663 (2001).

Miracci, Rosemarie A., Comment: *"Wisconsin v. Mitchell:* Punishable Conduct v. Punishable Thought," 21 New Engl. J. on Crim. & Civ. Confinement 131, 133 (1995).

Mueller, Abby, Comment: "Can Motive Matter? A Constitutional and Criminal Law Analysis of Motive in Hate Crime Legislation," 61 U.M.K.C. L. Rev. 619 (1993).

NOTE: "Toward a Constitutional Definition of Religion," 91 HARV. L. REV. 1056 [1978].

Ryan, Anne B., Comment: "Punishing Thought: A Narrative Deconstructing the Interpretive Dance of Hate Crime Legislation," 35 J. Marshall L. Rev. 123 (2001).

Sarno, Gregory G., ANNOTATION: "Regulation of Astrology, Clairvoyancy, Fortunetelling, and the Like," 91 A.L.R. 3rd 766 (2001).

Schwartz. Frederic S., "Making and Meeting the Prima Facie Case Under the Fair Housing Act," 20 Akron L. Rev. 291 (1986).

"Sect member on trial in son's death," *The Cape Cod Times,* June 3 2002, vol. 66, no. 132, page A4.

Seyferth, Paul D., "Evaluating Employment Discrimination Claims from a Defense Counsel's Perspective," 58 *Journal of the Missouri Bar* (2002), 268-272.

Smith, John M., NOTE & COMMENT: "Zoned for Residential Uses"—Like Prayer? Home Worship and Municipal Opposition in *LeBlanc-Sternberg v. Fletcher,*" 2000 B.Y. U.L. Rev 1153 (2000).

Wehener, Ann, "When a House is not a Home but a Church: A Proposal for Protection of Home Worship from Zoning Ordinances," 22 Ca. U.L. Rev. 491 (1993).

JOURNALS, PERIODICALS, AND ARTICLES—INTERNET

Barrette, Elizabeth, "Church of Ozark Avalon Wins Property Tax Case," http://www/ozarkavalon.org/property_tax_press_release.shtml.

Cooperman, Alan, "Lutheran Pastor suspended over interfaith meet: Missouri Synod wants apology for meeting with 'pagan clerics,'" *The San Francisco Chronicle,* July 5 2002, http://sfgate.com/dgi-bin/article/cqi?file=/c/a/2002/07/06/MN157497.DTL.

"Court Amends Indecency Charge for 'May King,'" *The Toledo Blade,* June 26 2001, http://nl3.newsbank.com/nl-search/we/Archives?p_action=list&p_topdoc=1; archived as Article ID: 0106260082.

Gearan, Anne, "Justices Refuse Case on Government Display of Ten Commandments," *Nando Times,* http://www.nandotimes.com/nation/storhy/16818p-310870c.html

Gettleman, Jeffrey, "Judge's Biblical Monument is Ruled Unconstitutional," *The New York Times,* November 19 2002, http://www.nytimes.com/2002/11/19/national/19COMM.html.

Goodstein, Laurie, "Bush's 'Jesus Day' Is Called a First Amendment Violation," *The New York Times*, http://www/nytimes.com/library/politics/camp/080600wh-bush-jesus.html.

"Government to ask rehearing of Pledge ruling: Judge stays Pledge decision pending appeals," http://www.cnn.com/2002/LAW/06/27/pledge.allegiance/. June 27 2002.

Harkavy, Ward, "Ashcroft to Christian Crowd: Use Government to Sell Jesus," *The Village Voice*, http://www.villagevoice.com/issues/0115/TheVillageVoiceharkavy.shtml.

U.S. Department of Housing and Urban Development, "Fair Housing: Equal Opportunity for All," www.hud.gov/fairhousing.

Hunter, George, "Teasing and taunting led girl to end her life: Pressures that prompted mass shootings also spur quiet suicides," *The Detroit News*, March 7 2001, http://www.detnews.com/2001/schools/0103/07/a01-196600.htm.

Jefferson, Thomas, "Autobiography, in reference to the Virginia Act for Religious Freedom," from a list of quotes compiled by Jim Walker, http://www.nobeliefs.com/jefferson.htm.

Kottke, Colleen, "Wiccan Chaplain Targeted by Attacks," *The Reporter*, http://www.wisinfo.com/thereporter/news/archive/local_7195409.shtml.

Kovacs, Joe, "Christmas in America becomes battleground: As holiday traditions draw national controversy, believers, pagans grapple over Jesus' inclusion," *WorldNetDaily*, December 14 2002, http://www.worldnetdaily.com/news/article.asp?ARTICLE_ID=29995.

"Lawsuit Challenges Discriminatory Prayer Policy of Chesterfield County Board of Supervisors: Rights Groups Say Prayer Policy Excludes Some Faiths, Violates Church-State Separation," http://www.au.org/press/pr021206.htm.

Michael, Robert, "FDR's Antisemitism," http://www.kimmel.net/fdr.html. 1998.

Martin, Peter W., "Introduction to Basic Legal Citation (LII 2002-2003 ed.)," http://www.law.cornell.edu/citation.

Mueller, Kara, "The School and the Ten Commandments," http: // revkara.com/originalworks/ten_commandments.html.

Norwood, Stacey, "Pagans Outrage Pell City Neighbors," wysiwg:// 4http://www.wiat.com/now/story/0,1597,225274-373,00.shtml.

Parish, Connie, "Officials Defend Nudist Camp's Permit Rejection," *The Leavenworth Times,* January 27 2002, http:// www.leavenworthtimes.com/archives/index.inn?loc=detail&doc=/ 2002/January/27-591-news5.txt;

Parish, Connie, "Camp's Neighbors Uncomfortable with Settlement," *The Leavenworth Times,* April 14 2002, http:// www.leavenworthtimes.com/archives/index.inn?loc=detail&doc=/ 2002/April/14-674-news2.txt.

"Religious Discrimination in U.S. State Constitutions," http:// www.religioustolerance.org/texas.htm.

Richmeier, John, "Planning Commission Votes Against Renewing Permit for Camp Gaea, Cites 'Morals' as Reason," *The Leavenworth Times,* from The Witches' Voice at http:// www.witchvox.com/wren/wn-detail.html?id=3481.

Smith, Denessa, "The Tempest Smith Foundation," http:// www.witchvox.com/wren/wn_detail.html?id=6272.

Swanson, Ian, "Pagan Scots turn backs on the Kirk," *Edinburgh News,* http://www.edinburghnews.com/index.cfm?id=538302002.

"Update: Camp Gaea and County Reach Agreement; Special Use Permit Granted," http://www.witchvox.com/wren/ wn_detail.html?id=4133.

Van Dine, Lynne, "Mother Wins Custody of Son, Even Though She Practices Animal Sacrifice," *Detroit News,* January 20 1994, http:// www.vix.com/pub/men/custody-divorce/cases/santa-ria.html.

Wehmeyer, Peggy, "Witches in Combat Boots: Pagan Rituals on Army Base Cast Controversial Spell," http://more.abcnews.go.com/ onair/closerlook/wnt990623_wehmeyer_story.html.

Williams, Jason, "Naked May King's Spring Rite to Result in Indecency Charge," *The Toledo Blade*, May 19 2001, http://nl3.newsbank.com/nl-search/we/Archives?p_action=list&p_topdoc=1; archive ID number 0105190109.

WEBSITES

http://www.acess.gpo.gov

http://www.aclu.org

http://www.americanreligion.org/cultwtch/polygamy.html

http://caag.state.ca.us/publications/civilrights/01CRhandbook/

http://www.campgaea.org/index.php?page=newsletter.

http://www.circlesanctuary.org/aboutcircle/circlehistory.html

http://www.law.cornell.edu/states/listing.html

http://www.law.cornell.edu/uscode

http://www.law.cornell.edu/rules/fre/overview.html

http:www.law.cornell.edu.rules/frcp/overview.html.

http://www.law.cornell.edu/topics/landlord_tenant.html

http://www.ssnx.com/courtrules

http://www/eeoc.gov

http://www.eeoc.gov/fact/qanda.html

http://www.law.emory.edu/FEDCTS/

http://expertpages.com/state_rules_of_evidence.htm

http://www.hud.gov

http://www.hud.gov/offices/fheo/FHLaws/FairHousing.Jan2002.pdf

http://www.martindale.com/

www.MassBar.org

http://www.milpagan.org

http://news.bbc.co.uk/hi/english/world/americas/newsid_1339000/1339341.stm

from http://nolo.com/lawcenter/ency/article.cfm/obj

http://www.sacredwell.org/ResourceArchives/General%20Interest/wiccans_in_the_army.htm

www.state.ma.us/dhcd

http://www.uscourts.gov/

MISCELLANEOUS

83 Am. Jur. 2d Zoning and Planning, Section 1.

39 AM. JUR. 684 Section 50.

110 C.M.R. 2.00. (Massachusetts).

29 C.F.R. Section 1605.1 (1990).

Massachusetts Department of Social Services. *Child Abuse and Neglect Reporting: A Guide for Mandated Reporters.*

———. *Child Protective Services: Parent's Guide.*

———. *Child Abuse Hurts Us All: Recognizing, Reporting and Preventing Child Abuse and Neglect.*

Department of the Army. Office of the Chief of Chaplains. *Religious Requirements and Practices of Certain Selected Groups: A Handbook for Chaplains.*

DODD 1300.17, "Accommodation of Religious Practices Within the Military Services," February 3, 1988 ASD (FM&P), through Ch. 1, October 17, 1988.

Oringderff, David L., Ph.D., and Lt. Col. U.S.A.F Ronald W. Schaefer, "Spiritual Philosophy and Practice of Wicca in the U.S. Military," The Sacred Well Congregation, Converse Texas (2001).

Oringderff, David L., Ph.D., "Cult Investigations: A Peace Officer's Handbook," Converse, Texas (1999).

Pagan Pride Project Press Release. October 14, 2002. Cecylyna Dewr, Executive Director, Pagan Pride Project.

INDEX

S

T

Z

ABOUT THE AUTHOR

D ana D. Eilers is a 1978 graduate of Smith College and a 1981 cum laude graduate of the New England School of Law, where she was published in the Law Review and served as one of its editors. She is a licensed attorney in the states of Illinois, Massachusetts, and Missouri. From 1982–1998, Dana practiced as a civil litigator with active trial firms in St. Louis, Missouri, and the bulk of her practice was in the states of Illinois and Missouri. She is currently retired from the practice of law and spends most of her year in Chatham, Massachusetts, where she is writing, teaching, and speaking. She is the author of the recent book *The Practical Pagan*, released in April, 2002 by Career Press/New Page Books.

Dana has been a practicing, eclectic Witch for approximately 20 years. Her personal spiritual tradition is inspired by Egyptian, Mayan, and Western European sources. She writes, teaches, and speaks on the topics of Witchcraft, Magic, Ritual, and Paganism. Her written works have appeared in *Green Egg, Pangaia, Sage Woman, Circle Sanctuary News*, and

Goodwitch Stories. More of her work can be found on The Witches' Voice (witchvox.com). She is a member of AREN's legal resource pool and of the OurFreedom list online where she serves as a resource and active voice for Pagan civil rights. She was the legal consultant to the joint project of WyrdWeavers Collective, the Pagan Educational Network, and the Covenant of Unitarian Universalist Pagans in the creation of the online pamphlet: *Pagan Leaders Denounce Religious Intolerance And Uphold The Constitution Of The United States Of America.* She was a member of the Papal Apology Committee and aided in the drafting of the Petition to the Pope to include Witches and Pagans in the Vatican speech given in January, 2000. She was a member of the BOILERPLATE committee, which formulated the letters and forms found at the Boilerplate Website. This site is for Pagans who wish to write coherent letters regarding their faith to newspapers, congressional leaders, etc.

She is originally from St. Louis, Missouri, where she addressed the public through the media: radio, television, and the newspapers regarding Witchcraft and Paganism. In St. Louis, she created and facilitated Conversations with Pagans, a forum where the Pagan curious, the Pagan friendly, and the Pagan folk can discuss all topics of interest. Dana has presented this forum at many different events and in different places all over the country. For years, she has taught classes regarding Wicca, Magick, and ritual. For many years, she served on the Ritual Committee for both the Pagan Picnic and Magickal Weekend. As such, she helped to create and perform public ritual for groups ranging in size from less than a dozen to approximately 250. She was a co-founder of the Occasional Coven in St. Louis. In the St. Louis area, Dana worked to create a large, thriving and public Pagan community. She is a founding member of the Omnistic Fellowship, a religious fellowship with a particular focus on alternative spirituality and a founding member of the Council for Alternative Spiritual Traditions (CAST), which is a Pagan leadership council. She served for four years as the Chair of the Steering Committee for WildHaven, a four-day Pagan Festival celebrating the Autumnal Equinox and was one of the founders of WildHaven. She worked and practiced both in coven and as a Solitary.

In Massachusetts, she has appeared on several radio programs on WOMR Outermost Radio in Provincetown, and she has been featured in articles in *The Cape Cod Chronicle* and *The Cape Cod Times*. She is a regular panelist on the radio program Radio Omnibus' "Cabin in the Pines Roundtable of the Air," hosted by Christopher Hawley, and airing on WOMR Outermost Radio, FM 92.1, in Provincetown, Massachusetts. Her radio appearances have also included an interview with Duke Skorich on the Duke Skorich show, NPR, 91.3 FM and 102.9 FM; Website at KUWS.FM. In October of 2000, she presented and facilitated a public ritual for Womens' Week in Provincetown, Massachusetts, and gave a seminar in Goddess-centered spirituality. She has presented the Ritual of Wands as healing ritual on several occasions for the Cape Cod Pagan community and continues to facilitate Conversations With Pagans in her community upon request. Currently, she works both in Circle and as a Solitary. She continues to create and to perform public rituals.

Dana can be reached via email at: revdana@MindSpring.com

CONVERSATIONS WITH PAGANS

Created in the early 1990s, this open conversational forum was created and developed by Dana D. Eilers as a means of public outreach, communication, education, and community building. It is a forum where Pagans, the Pagan friendly, and the Pagan curious can come together and discuss topics of mutual interest. In the St. Louis area, Conversations With Pagans ran once a month for nearly six years at Mystic Valley. Dana presented this forum at WildHaven, the Pagan Picnic, Convocation, Invocation, Magickal Weekend, at The Chatham Herbary in Chatham, Massachusetts, and for the Brewster, Massachusetts Covenant of the Unitarian Universalist Pagans group. She has served as a facilitator for the Pagan Town Meeting at one of the Massachusetts Pagan Pride events. The format for Conversations With Pagans is simple, and it is designed to encourage everyone to participate. The forum begins with a round robin introduction of the attendees: that is, everyone introduces themselves in 10 sentences or less, and then, the floor is open for conversation.

Dana rarely sets a topic, but has been known to do that when there is a particularly keen interest in a certain topic. Participants in the conversation must raise their hand in order to take the floor and while one person has the floor, others are encouraged to respect the speaker by waiting their turn to speak. Topics of conversation have varied widely from "Seen any good Pagan type movies lately" to "How do you reverse a spell" to "Do you people really worship the Devil?"

PUBLICATIONS

The Practical Pagan, by Dana D. Eilers. Career Press/New Page Books, Franklin Lakes, N.J. (2002). ISBN 1-56414-601-4.

Pangaia, Issue no. 29, Autumn, 2001, article entitled "Finding Ella: A Witch Goes in Search of her Family Heritage," pages 18-22.

Pangaia, Issue no. 29, Autumn, 2001, "Faith-based Funding: Should Pagan organizations accept government money? Yes!" pages 15-16.

Pangaia, Issue No. 27, Spring, 2001, article entitled "Creating a Common Vision: Five Ways to Seed and Cultivate Your Own Community," pages 40, 42.

Green Egg, July/August, 1999, article entitled "The Crystal Siefferly Case: Anatomy of a Law Suit," pages 20-22.

Sage Woman, Winter, 1997, article entitled "He Who Sleeps Behind the Door," pages 21-15.

Circle Sanctuary News, Spring, 1996, article entitled "Out of the Basement: Weaving the Tapestry of Pagan Culture."

Goodwitch Stories, Summer, 1995, short story entitled "Elder Brother," pages 7-9.

Goodwitch Stories, Winter, 1995-1995, poem entitled "We Witches Wait."

Sage Woman, Summer, 1993, article entitled "Beyond Fear," pages 14-15.

MEDIA (TELEVISION, RADIO, AND PRINT)

Wood, Tim, "The Practical Pagan Comes to Town: Chatham Woman Pens Commonsense Guide for Modern Pagans," May 30, 2002 *The Cape Cod Chronicle*, page 29.

December 13, 2001, interview with Duke Skorich on the Duke Skorich show, NPR, 91.3 FM and 102.9 FM; Website at KUWS.FM.

Regular panelist on Radio Omnibus' "Cabin in the Pines Roundtable of the Air," with host Christopher Hawley and other guests, featured on WOMR Outermost Radio, FM 92.1, Provincetown, Massachusetts.

May, 2001, interview with Joe Poire on "The Joe Poire Show," WOMR Outermost Radio, FM 92.1, Provincetown, Massachusetts.

January, 2001, two interviews with Dr. Paula Sperry on WOMR Outermost Radio, FM 92.1, Provincetown, Massachusetts.

September 27, 2000, interview with Tim Wood of *The Cape Cod Chronicle.*

June 22, 2001, Interview with Marjorie Morningstar on WOMR, Outermost Radio, Provincetown, Massachusetts .

October 31, 1998, THE ST. LOUIS POST DISPATCH, article entitled "For Pagans, Halloween is a serious, Sacred Time of Magic," by Chris Carroll.

October 7, 1998, KPLR TV, WB Channel 11 News, interview with Christine Buck.

October 31-November 6, 1997, *Webster-Kirkwood Times*, article entitled "A Very Pagan All Hallows Eve," by Don Corrigan.

June, 1996, radio interview for KDHX FM 88, St. Louis Missouri, program entitled "Out and Open," hosted by Amy Doll and Linda Serafini.

October 1995, *The St. Louis Post Dispatch*, article entitled "Special Days Honor Dead: Christians, Pagans Remember Saints, Souls, Spirits, by Kathryn Rodgers.

August 9-15, 1995, *St. Louis Riverfront Times*, article entitled "Pagan Offerings, by Jeanette Batz.

July 26, 1995, *The St Louis Post Dispatch*, article entitled "Pagans Plan Picnic to Celebrate Beliefs," by Ellen Ellick.

July 25, 1994, *The St Louis Post Dispatch*, full frontal photograph of me calling the Southern Quarter at the Opening Ritual to the Pagan Picnic, with caption reading "Proudly Pagan."

March, April 1994, *The Pathfinder*, article entitled "Wicca: A Look at Modern Practice."

December, 1992, *St. Louis Riverfront Times*, featured in a column written by William Stage and entitled "Mississippi Mud."

Resources on the Web

For The Witches' Voice

"Some Brief Points for Modern Pagans," at http://www.witchvox.com/white/paganismanlaw.html.

"Hurston v. Henderson, 2001 WL 65204: A Case Analysis," at http://www.witchvox.com/white/hvh.html.

"Definitely NOT Like in the Movies: A Response to the Teen Pagans Among Us," http://www.witchvox.com/words/words_1999/ e_notinthemovies1.html.

"Santa Fe Independent School District v. Doe: An Analysis" http://www.witchvox.com/white/santafevdoe.html.

http://www.witchvox.com/cases/abrahamsen.html.

The Wiccanpagan Times

"Samhain in the Aftermath of September 11, 2001." (This article was published as part of their October celebration, and you may have to contact Boudica to get the cite for it.)

Legal Comments

http://www.kriselda.net/candlestar/RelFree/DanaDettmer.htm.

Contributions to Websites and Other Online Publications

http:www.bloomington.in.us/~pen/boilerplate.html.
http://www.wiccauk.com/articles/publicritual.html.